DISCARDED

D1065210

Rain Forests
of the
World

Rain Forests
of the
World

Volume 11
Index

MARSHALL CAVENDISH
NEW YORK • LONDON • TORONTO • SYDNEY

R
j577.34
Rai
v.11

Marshall Cavendish Corporation
99 White Plains Road
Tarrytown, New York
10591-9001

Website: www.marshallcavendish.com

©2002 Marshall Cavendish Corporation

All rights reserved. No part of this book may be reproduced or utilized in any form or by any means, electronic or mechanical, including photocopying, recording, or by any information storage and retrieval system, without prior written permission from the publisher and the copyright holders.

Consulting Editors: Rolf E. Johnson, Nathan E. Kraucunas

Contributing Authors: Theresa Greenaway, Jill Bailey, Michael Chinery, Malcolm Penny, Mike Linley, Philip Steele, Chris Oxlade, Ken Preston-Mafham, Rod Preston-Mafham, Clare Oliver, Don Birchfield

Discovery Books
    Managing Editor: Paul Humphrey
    Project Editor: Gianna Williams
    Text Editor: Valerie Weber
    Designer: Ian Winton
    Cartographer: Stefan Chabluk
    Illustrators: Jim Channell, Stuart Lafford, Christian Webb, Kevin Maddison

Marshall Cavendish
    Editor: Marian Armstrong
    Editorial Director: Paul Bernabeo

(cover) *Sumatran Tiger*
(frontispiece) *Scarlet Macaw*

Editor's Note: Many systems of dating have been used by different cultures throughout history. *Rain Forests of the World* uses B.C.E. (Before Common Era) and C.E. (Common Era) instead of B.C. (Before Christ) and A.D. (Anno Domini, "In the Year of Our Lord") out of respect for the diversity of the world's peoples.

Library of Congress Cataloging-in-Publication Data
Rain forests of the world.
                v. cm.
        Includes bibliographical references and index.
        Contents: v. 1. Africa-bioluminescence — v. 2. Biomass-clear-cutting — v. 3. Climate and weather-emergent — v. 4. Endangered species-food web — v. 5. Forest fire-iguana — v .6. Indonesia-manatee — v. 7. Mangrove forest-orangutan — v. 8. Orchid-red panda — v. 9. Reforestation-spider — v. 10. Squirrel-Yanomami people — v. 11. Index.
            ISBN 0-7614-7254-1 (set)
                1. Rain forests—Encyclopedias.   1. Marshall Cavendish Corporation.
        QH86 .R39 2002
        578.734—dc21

    ISBN 0-7614-7254-1 (set)
    ISBN 0-7614-7265-7 (vol. 11)

Printed and bound in Italy

07 06 05 04 03 02   6 5 4 3 2 1

Contents

Glossary

Aboriginal: the first of a kind known to exist in a particular country or area.

Afrikaans: the mother tongue of Afrikaners, South African settlers of Dutch descent.

Algae: plantlike organisms that produce their own food by photosynthesis but do not have proper stems, leaves, and veins.

Amazonia: the vast region in South America drained by the Amazon River.

Ambush: to lie in wait for prey, usually well concealed, and then take it by surprise when it comes within reach.

Amphibian: a creature that may spend most of its life on land but must return to water to breed.

Anesthetic: a chemical that numbs the tissues so that an animal feels no pain.

Anthropologist: a scientist that studies human societies, past and present.

Antibiotic: a substance that prevents bacteria from multiplying.

Anti-inflammatory: a substance that prevents inflammation in the body, which is characterized by pain, heat, and redness.

Aphid: a small sluggish insect with sucking mouthparts that commonly sucks the juices of plants.

Aquatic: an animal or plant that lives in water.

Arboreal: an animal that spends most of its life in the trees.

Archaeologist: someone who excavates ancient remains and studies them scientifically.

Aril: a covering or sheath found on certain seeds.

Aroid: a large family of plants with broad, glossy, deep green leaves, many of which occur in the rain forest understory.

Assimilate: to give up one's customs in order to live like people in the dominant culture.

Autonomy: a group of people that govern themselves; also, the right to self-govern.

Bacteria: a tiny organism, one of the smallest forms of life, that may be made up of a single cell or many cells.

Beds: prepared areas of soil used for sowing seeds or planting seedlings or cuttings.

Binocular vision: the coordinated use of both eyes to judge with great accuracy the size of an object and its distance.

Biodiversity: a shortened term for biological diversity, which describes the variety of plants and animals in an area.

Biologist: a scientist who studies biology, the science of living things.

Bioluminescent: the ability of an animal to produce light as the result of a chemical reaction within its body.

Biomass: a measure of the amount of living matter (both animals and plants) in a certain area.

Biome: a large area that is distinguished by its climate and vegetation. Tropical rain forest is one type of biome, desert is another kind of biome.

Brachiation: when an animal propels itself through the trees by swinging its arms.

Bromeliad: any of over one thousand plants of the pineapple family that have a crown of stiff, spiny leaves. Some bromeliads grow on the ground, but most of them are epiphytes.

Bush meat: the flesh of wild animals killed for food.

Caboclo: a mixed-race riverside settler in Amazonia, descended from European (mainly Portuguese) settlers and the local Indian population.

Caecilian: a long, thin, legless amphibian that at first glance resembles a large earthworm.

Camouflage: a form of trickery or deception, particularly one involving the use of concealing colors and patterns, enabling an animal to avoid the attention of its enemies or its prey.

Canines: sharp teeth at the front corners of the mouth, used for piercing food or for killing prey.

Cannibalism: the act of catching and eating members of one's own species.

Canopy: the "roof" of the forest, composed of interlocking tree branches that cut off most of the light to the forest floor.

Carbohydrate: any of a wide range of substances consisting entirely of carbon, hydrogen, and oxygen. Glucose is one of the simplest carbohydrates. Energy-rich foods such as cane sugar, sucrose, and starch have a more complex structure than glucose. Cellulose, which is a plant's main building material, is a complex carbohydrate.

Carbon dioxide: a gas that makes up less than one part per thousand of the air around us. It is essential for plants because they cannot make their food without it.

Carnivore: a meat-eating animal or plant.

Carpel: the female part of a flower that gives rise to the fruit and seeds after pollination.

Carrion: dead animal remains.

Cartilage: a dense tissue that covers the surfaces of bones at the joints, protecting them from being damaged by rubbing against each other.

Cataract: a waterfall.

Catchment area: the area of land from which rainfall flows into a particular system of rivers.

Cellulose: a white chemical substance that forms the walls of plant cells and gives shape to the plant.

Chitin: a very hard hornlike substance that forms the external skeleton of insects, spiders, and crustaceans and is present in the cell walls of fungi.

Chlorofluorocarbon: a greenhouse gas that contains chlorine, fluorine, and carbon.

Chlorophyll: the green substance inside a plant that converts sunlight into energy.

Cilia: threadlike organs that project out from the body of a cell.

Clear-cutting: the cutting down of all of the trees in an area of forest.

Compost: rotting vegetation that has reached a finely divided state.

Condensation: water produced by mist or steam when it cools.

Confiscation: taking something away as a punishment for breaking the law.

Coniferous: trees with needle-shaped leaves and cones instead of flowers.

Corrugated iron: sheet metal formed into ridges for strength; used as a building material.

Cretaceous: the period of geological time from about 144 to 65 million years ago, during which the dinosaurs dominated Earth and mammals and flowering plants spread across the land.

Crop: a soft, baglike part of the digestive system where a bird stores food before it is crushed by the gizzard and digested in the stomach.

Cuticle: the outer layer of an organism. It is usually made up of dead cells impregnated with waterproofing waxes and a tough substance like chitin (invertebrates) or keratin (vertebrates) that also helps prevent the entry of bacteria and fungi.

Deciduous: falling out or off at a certain time of year, such as the fall of leaves in autumn.

Decimate: to destroy most of something.

Decomposition: the process of decay that begins when animals and plants die.

Deforestation: the destruction of forest trees by felling or burning to create land for farming, ranching, mining, and towns.

Dengue fever: a tropical disease that causes terrible fevers and a rash but is seldom fatal.

Dismember: to tear something to pieces.

Diurnal: active during the day (as opposed to *nocturnal* which means active during the night).

Drought: a period of very dry weather when rain fails to arrive.

Dry forest: forests with a long dry season and often only little rainfall.

Dry rain forest: a type of subtropical rain forest found in sheltered areas in which there is 24–43 inches (600–1,100 mm) of rainfall a year and a marked dry season.

Ecological niche: the range of habitat conditions and resources in which a particular species is able to live.

Economics: the way in which labor, goods, and money are used and managed in society.

Ecosystem: a group of plants and animals that interact with each other in an area (called their environment). A single tree and a whole forest are both ecosystems.

Electroplate: that part of an electric eel's electric organ that produces the electricity, made of a thin sheet of muscle. There are around five thousand electroplates in each electric organ.

Emissions: gases released into the atmosphere when fossil fuels are burned in power plants or in engines.

Enclave: a small pocket of a particular type of territory that is surrounded by a different type of territory.

Endemic: a living organism that comes from just one or a few particular areas of the world and is not naturally found anywhere else.

Enzyme: a substance that assists in chemical changes without itself being used up in the process.

Epiphyte: a name given to any plant that grows on another without taking any food from it. Most epiphytes grow on trees.

Estuary: a water passage where a river meets the sea.

Ethnobotanist: a person who studies the traditional uses of plants by native tribes, usually for medicine, sometimes for food or clothing.

Evaporation: the process by which a liquid turns into a vapor (gas).

Evolution: the process by which living organisms change from one form to another over a long period of time.

Excretion: something that has been pushed out or has seeped out.

Exoskeleton: a hard outer covering that protects the soft bodies of invertebrates such as insects, spiders, crustaceans, and shellfish.

Extinction: the final dying out of an animal or plant species.

Fang: a spider's jaw or one of the enlarged teeth of a snake that are used to inject venom into prey.

Fauna: animal life.

Feral: a wild animal that is descended from domestic animals.

Fledge: the stage when a young bird is able to fly and is therefore ready to leave the nest.

Floodplain: a flat area on either side of a river onto which the river floods during periods of heavy rain.

Flora: plant life.

Fossil: the remains of an animal, usually only the bones, preserved with minerals and turned to rock.

Fossil fuel: a fuel made deep underground over millions of years from the remains of ancient animals and plants. Oil, coal, and natural gas are fossil fuels.

Fruiting body: that part of a fungus that is normally produced above ground for the purpose of producing spores. What we call mushrooms and toadstools are fungal fruiting bodies.

Gene: a tiny fragment of genetic material in the nucleus of a plant or animal cell. It controls one or more characteristics of the plant or animal.

Germinate: when seeds sprout and start to grow.

Global warming: the gradual warming up of the earth's atmosphere, believed to be due to increasing amounts of carbon dioxide in the air.

Grub: a larva with no legs. Grubs can be the larvae of bees, wasps, or many types of beetles.

Guerrilla: a member of a small fighting force that moves about an area attacking conventional military forces and carrying out acts of sabotage and terrorism.

Hardwood timber: timber from slow-growing trees, whose close grain makes it ideal for furniture and carving.

Head-hunting: the practice of removing the heads of enemies as trophies of warfare.

Hemisphere: half of the globe or world.

Herbaceous: plants that have soft stems with no woody component.

Herbivorous: feeding entirely on plants or vegetable matter.

Hierarchy: the system of ranking in communities of animals or birds, in which each animal knows its own status in relation to the others.

Humidity: a measure of the amount of water vapor held by the atmosphere.

Humus: the decomposed remains of plant material.

Hunter-gatherer: someone who lives by hunting animals and gathering fruits and roots to eat.

Hydroelectricity: electricity generated by the power of flowing water.

Immunity: the ability of the body to resist disease and infection.

Inbreeding: mating between two animals that are closely related.

Incisors: the front teeth, usually flat or spade-shaped, used for cutting and nibbling.

Incubate: the development and hatching process of eggs in the presence of heat.

Indigenous: a plant or animal living in its native land.

Infectious: a disease that is passed from person to person in water supplies, by insect or other animal, or by physical contact.

Influenza: a very contagious disease caused by a virus. Its symptoms include headaches, fever, aching joints, and breathing difficulties.

Infrared: a type of heat radiation that comes from hot objects. It is how heat reaches the earth from the sun and what you feel when the sun's rays warm your face.

Insoluble: something that cannot be dissolved in water.

Invertebrate: an animal that lacks a spinal column (backbone). Some invertebrates, such as insects, have a hard outer shell.

Irrigate: to supply extra water from streams, rivers, lakes, ponds, or reservoirs to agricultural land.

Isthmus: a narrow fringe or strip of land.

Larva (pl. larvae): a young insect that is markedly different from the adult and that has to pass through a pupal or chrysalis stage to reach maturity.

Lassa fever: a highly-lethal viral disease.

Latex: a sticky liquid that oozes out of some plants when their stems are cut; the white, sticky sap of a rubber tree.

Latitude: the distance, measuring north and south, of a place from the equator, which is at 0° latitude.

Leach: when a liquid percolates through material.

Leishmaniasis: a group of three different diseases that are caused by different parasites, and that are transmitted to humans by sandfly bites.

Leukemia: a disease in which the body produces far too many white blood cells.

Liana: a climbing plant with long tendrils that grows up trees to support itself and reach sunlight.

Malaria: a human disease caused by a single-celled animal living in the red blood cells.

Mangrove: any one of many kinds of shrubs and trees that grow in muddy tidal areas along coasts and up tidal rivers, mainly in the Tropics.

Maori: the people who are indigenous to New Zealand.

Marsupial: a mammal whose young are born very small and helpless after a brief pregnancy and that complete their development attached to their mother's teats, usually in a pouch called a marsupium.

Metamorphosis: a process in which an animal makes a complete change in its shape, appearance, and behavior as it grows to adulthood, i.e., from a tadpole to a frog or a caterpillar into a butterfly.

Microbe: a microscopic organism, especially bacteria that cause disease.

Microorganism: an organism (living creature) too small to see without the aid of a microscope.

Mimicry: the copying of the shape, color, or behavior of one living organism by another.

Molecule: the smallest particle of an element or compound, and made up of atoms.

Mollusk: any member of the large group of invertebrate animals that includes cockles, slugs, and snails. They all have soft bodies that are generally enclosed in a protective shell.

Molt: when animals shed their skins in order to develop a stage further.

Monsoon: a wind that results in a period of very heavy rains that fall on parts of India and Southeast Asia between April and September.

Monsoon forest: certain forests in Asia that have a long dry season and then a long spell of heavy rain.

Nectar: the sweet liquid produced in flowers and sometimes elsewhere on plants. It attracts insects and other animals.

Nectary: a patch of cells in a plant that secrete the sweet, sugary liquid known as nectar. Nectaries usually occur in the flowers, often at the bases of the petals, but also occur on the leaves and stems of some plants.

Neotropical: species that live in the Tropics of the New World (the Americas).

Niche: the range of habitat conditions and resources in which a particular species is able to live.

Nitrate: a mineral salt that contains nitrogen and oxygen. Nitrates are soluble in water, so they are important sources of nitrogen for plants.

Nocturnal: active during the night.

Nomadic: continually wandering from place to place, with no settled home.

Nucleus (pl. nuclei): a tiny structure inside all animal and plant cells. It controls what the cell does and contains genetic material.

Nutrient: any substance used as food by living things.

Nymph: the immature stage of a variety of insects that undergo a simple metamorphosis from young to adult form. The nymph is generally similar to the adult and does not pass through a pupal stage to get to its adult state.

Omnivorous: an animal that eats both meat and vegetable matter.

Ore: a rock or mineral from which a metal can be extracted. For example, the mineral bauxite is the main ore of aluminum.

Organism: any living creature, including both animals and plants.

Ovipositor: the egg-laying part of a female insect.

Oxbow lake: a piece of landlocked river that is left behind when a river changes its course.

Palpus (pl. palps): a pair of appendages that are sensitive to touch and taste. Spiders use them the same way that insects use their antennae.

Parasite: an organism (plant or animal) that lives off another living organism without benefiting that organism.

Peninsula: an area of land almost completely surrounded by water that is attached to a larger area of land.

Pharmaceutical: used in the preparation of medicines.

Phosphate: mineral compounds that contain phosphorus and oxygen, derived from the breakdown of rocks to form soil. Phosphates are involved in the energy-generating processes of all living things and form many substances in cells.

Photosynthesis: the process by which green plants use the energy in sunlight to make sugar from carbon dioxide and water.

Phylogeny: the evolutionary history of a plant or animal: what its ancestors were.

Pistil: the part of a flower to which pollen grains stick.

Placenta: an organ that develops in many mammals to link a developing fetus to its mother's womb.

Plantain: a large, starchy type of banana, commonly used for cooking.

Plywood: board made by gluing several thin sheets of timber together in such a way that the grain of one sheet runs at right angles to the grain of the next sheet. This gives the board extra strength.

Pneumatic: inflated with air.

Poacher: a person who hunts or steals animals that are protected by law.

Pollen: the dustlike material produced by flowers. When carried to another flower by animals or the wind, it triggers the formation of seeds.

Pollination: the transfer of pollen from the stamens to the stigmas of flowers.

Polygamy: the practice of a person being married to more than one other person at a time.

Predator: any animal that kills other animals for food.

Prehensile: a limb that is able to grasp like a hand.

Primate: any type of mammal with a relatively large brain, hands and feet that can grasp things (often with opposable thumbs or big toes), usually five fingers and toes with flattened nails instead of claws, and good eyesight.

Proboscis: the name given to the slender tongue of a butterfly or moth, and also to the piercing beaks of some other insects.

Propagation: the reproduction of plants either as a natural process or by sowing seeds or taking cuttings.

Protozoan: common name for any microscopic, single-celled animal.

Pulp: wood that has been treated so that its fibers separate out; used to make paper.

Pupa: the stage in an insect's life cycle when the tissues of the larva (grub or caterpillar) are replaced by those of the adult. Pupae are usually encased in a hard covering or a silk cocoon.

Quassia: a tree that produces a bitter medicinal tonic and insecticide.

Rabies: a disease caused by a virus that affects the nervous system and unless treated at an early stage is always fatal.

Regurgitate: to bring up food from the stomach after being swallowed.

Rehabilitation: the care of an injured animal, with the ultimate aim of releasing it back into the wild.

Reproductive system: that part of a plant or animal that is involved in the production of offspring.

Respiration: the process by which animals and plants take in oxygen and use it to turn sugars into energy for movement and growth. A by-product of animal respiration is carbon dioxide.

Rheumatism: a severe inflammation of the joints and muscles that causes stiffness and pain.

Rhizome: a creeping underground stem, often swollen with stored food.

Rosette: a circular pattern of markings arranged rather like the petals of a rose.

Rut: the mating season for deer, when males fight to establish the right to mate with the females.

Sacramental: of importance in religious ceremony.

Scavenger: a creature that feeds mainly on the remains of dead plants or animals.

Secondary rain forest: new growth of plants and trees that fills a small area of forest that had been cleared.

Sexual reproduction: the production of the next generation of a living organism by means of mating between male and female animals or by pollination in plants.

Shoal: a sandbank or shallow water.

Silt: soil washed off the land and down rivers in areas of heavy rainfall.

Slash-and-burn: a form of agriculture that involves cutting down all the trees in a given area and then burning whatever is left. The land is then used for farming, benefiting in the short-term from the nutrients released by the burned vegetation.

Social insect: an insect species that lives in a colony containing numerous individuals with different tasks. All the insects work for the good of the whole community.

Solitary insect: an insect species where individuals do not group up to form complex societies.

Spinneret: any of the slender appendages at the rear of a spider's body through which the silk emerges. Most spiders have six spinnerets.

Spore: a minute, dustlike reproductive cell produced by mosses, liverworts, ferns, and fungi.

Stamen: the part of a flower that produces pollen.

Staple food: the main, usually starchy, food eaten by a group of people.

Starch: a complex chemical that provides the main food storage cells in plants. Many human foodstuffs are made from the starches of plants such as potatoes and grains.

Stigma: the part of the carpel (the female part of the flower) that receives pollen grains during pollination. A flower with a single carpel has a single stigma; a flower with several carpels will have a stigma on each one.

Subtropical: describes areas with a tropical climate and habitat but that lie just outside the Tropics, i.e., north of the Tropic of Cancer and south of the Tropic of Capricorn.

Surface tension: the thin, skinlike coating on the surface of water when water meets air.

Synchronize: to happen or make happen at exactly the same time.

Tannins: defensive bitter chemicals found in the bark, leaves, and fruits of many rain forest trees.

Temperate rain forest: forests with high rainfall in the temperate regions of the world that have a distinct winter and summer.

Terrestrial: an animal or plant that lives on land.

Thorax: the part of the body between the neck and abdomen of an invertebrate.

Topsoil: the upper layers and surface of the soil, in which plants take root.

Trade wind: a wind that blows toward the equator from the northeast and southeast. It is caused by hot air rising at the equator.

Transpiration: to lose water by evaporation.

Tributary: a small stream or river which flows into a larger stream or river.

Tropics: the regions on either side of the equator that remain warm throughout the year.

Tundra: a flat area of the Arctic where the soil is permanently frozen.

Ultraviolet: a kind of radiation just beyond the violet end of the light spectrum. It is present in sunlight but invisible to human eyes. Many animals, such as insects, can see it.

Understory: the layer of trees and shrubs between the forest floor and the canopy.

Vegetarian: an animal that eats only plant food; also known as a herbivore.

Venom: a poison that is injected into another animal in some way—usually through fangs or stings. It may be used for defense or to kill or paralyze prey.

Vertebrate: an animal that possesses a backbone or vertebrae.

Watershed: an area drained by a river.

Further Reading and Research

Internet Sites

Visit these websites for more information:

Passport to the Rainforest at http://passporttoknowledge.com/rainforest/main.html

Rainforest Action Network at http://www.ran.org/kids_action/

The Rainforest-Alliance at http://www.rainforest-alliance.org/kids&teachers/index.html

The Rainforest Workshop at http://kids.osd.wednet.edu/Marshall/rainforest_home_page.html

Science in the Rainforest at http://www.pbs.org/tal/costa_rica/rainwalk.html

World Wide Fund for Nature at http://www.panda.org/kids/wildlife/idxtrpmn.htm

Yahoo's Rain Forest Links for Kids at
http://yahooligans.com/Science_and_Oddities/The_Earth/Ecology/Rainforests

Zoom Rainforest at http://www.enchantedlearning.com/subjects/rainforest/

Books

Albert, Toni. *The Remarkable Rainforest: An Active-Learning Book for Kids.* Mechanicsburg, PA: Trickle Creek Books, 1996.

Behler, Deborah A. *The Rain Forest of the Pacific Northwest (Ecosystems of North America).* Tarrytown, NY: Benchmark Books, 2000.

Cheshire, Gerard. *Nature Unfolds The Tropical Rainforest (Nature Unfolds).* New York: Crabtree Publishers, 2001.

Chinery, Michael. *People and Places (Secrets of the Rainforest).* New York: Crabtree Publishers, 2000.

Chinery, Michael. *Plants and Planteaters (Secrets of the Rainforest).* New York: Crabtree Publishers, 2000.

Chinery, Michael. *Resources and Conservation (Secrets of the Rainforest).* New York: Crabtree Publishers, 2000.

Deiters, Erika and Jim Deiters. *Tree Frogs (Animals of the Rain Forest).* Austin, TX: Raintree/Steck-Vaughn, 2001.

Dollar, Sam. *Anteaters (Animals of the Rain Forest).* Austin, TX: Raintree/Steck-Vaughn, 2001.

Dubosque, Doug. *Draw! Rainforest Animals*. Molalla, OR: Peel Productions, 1994.

Fowler, Allan. *Save the Rain Forests*. New York: Children's Press, 1996.

Fredericks, Anthony. *Exploring the Rain Forest: Science Activities for Kids*. Golden, CO: Fulcrum Publishers, 1996.

George, Michael. *Rain Forest (Images)*. Mankato, MN: Creative Education, 1997.

Gibbons, Gail. *Nature's Green Umbrella: Tropical Rain Forests*. New York: William Morrow & Company, 1994.

Gidwitz, Tom. *Story in the Stone: The Formation of a Tropical Land Bridge (Rain Forest Pilot)*. Austin, TX: Raintree/Steck-Vaughn, 2000.

Goodman, Susan. *Adventures in the Amazon Rain Forest: Ultimate Field Trip (Ultimate Field Trip, No. 1)*. New York: Aladdin Paperbacks, 1999.

Harris, Nicholas. *Into the Rainforest: One Book Makes Hundreds of Pictures of Rainforest Life (The Ecosystems Xplorer)*. Alexandria, VA: Time Life, 1996.

Johnson, Rebecca L. *A Walk in the Rain Forest*. Minneapolis, MN: Carolrhoda Books, 2000.

Kerven, Rosalind. *The Rain Forest Storybook: Traditional Stories from the Original Forest Peoples of South America, Africa, and South-East Asia*. New York: Cambridge University Press, 1994.

Kite, Lorien. *A Rain Forest Tree (Small Worlds)*. New York: Crabtree Publishers, 1999.

Knight, Tim. *Journey into the Rainforest*. New York: Oxford University Press Children's Books, 2001.

Lalley, Pat. *Jaguars (Animals of the Rain Forest)*. Austin, TX: Raintree/Steck-Vaughn, 2000.

Landau, Elaine. *Tropical Rain Forests Around the World (First Book)*. New York: Franklin Watts, Incorporated, 1991.

Lasky, Kathryn. *The Most Beautiful Roof in the World: Exploring the Rainforest Canopy*. San Diego, CA: Harcourt Brace & Company, 1997.

MacDonald, Fiona. *Rainforest (Topic Books)*. New York: Franklin Watts, Incorporated, 2000.

McCormick, Rosie. *Rain Forest Worlds (Discovery Guide)*. Princeton, NJ: Two-Can Publishers, 2001.

Morgan, Sally. *Saving the Rain Forest (Earth Watch)*. New York: Franklin Watts, Incorporated, 1999.

Oldfield, Sara. *Rain Forests (Endangered People and Places)*. Minneapolis, MN: Lerner Publications Company, 1996.

Osborne, Will and Mary Pope Osborne. *Rain Forests (Magic Tree House Research Guide)*. New York: Random House, 2001.

Pandell, Karen. *Journey Through the Northern Rainforest*. New York: Dutton Children's Books, 1999.

Parker, Edward and Anna Lewington. *People of the Rain Forests*. Austin, TX: Raintree/Steck Vaughn, 1998.

Pascoe, Elaine. *Mysteries of the Rain Forest: 20th Century Medicine Man (The New Explorers)*. Woodbridge, CT: Blackbirch Marketing, 1998.

Patent, Dorothy Hinshaw. *Children Save the Rain Forest*. New York: Cobblehill Books/Dutton, 1996.

Pipes, Rose. *Rain Forests (World Habitats)*. Austin, TX: Raintree/Steck Vaughn, 1998.

Pirotta, Saviour. *People in the Rain Forest (Deep in the Rain Forest)*. Austin, TX: Raintree/Steck-Vaughn, 1999.

Pirotta, Saviour. *Predators in the Rain Forest (Deep in the Rain Forest)*. Austin, TX: Raintree/Steck-Vaughn, 1999.

Pirotta, Saviour. *Rivers in the Rain Forest (Deep in the Rain Forest)*. Austin, TX: Raintree/Steck-Vaughn, 1999.

Pirotta, Saviour. *Trees and Plants in the Rain Forest (Deep in the Rain Forest)*. Austin, TX: Raintree/Steck-Vaughn, 1999.

Ricciuti, Edward R. *Rainforest (Biomes of the World)*. Tarrytown, NY: Benchmark Books, 1996.

Riley, Peter D., Sherry Gerstein, and Barry Croucher. *Nightwatch: Nightlife in the Tropical Rainforest: Windows on Science Series*. Pleasantville, NY: Readers Digest, 1999.

Ross, Kathy. *Crafts for Kids Who Are Wild About Rainforests*. Brookfield, CT: Millbrook Press, 1997.

Sauvain, Philip. *Rain Forests (Geography Detective)*. Minneapolis, MN: Carolrhoda Books, 1997.

Savage, Steven. *Animals of the Rain Forest*. Austin, TX: Raintree/Steck-Vaughn, 1999.

Sayre, April Pulley. *Tropical Rain Forest (Exploring Earth's Biomes)*. New York: Twenty First Century Books, 1995.

Senior, Kathryn. *Rain Forest (Fast Forward)*. New York: Franklin Watts, Incorporated, 1999.

Steele, Christy. *Anacondas (Animals of the Rain Forest)*. Austin, TX: Raintree/Steck-Vaughn, 2000.

Stille, Darlene R. *Tropical Rain Forests (True Books-Ecosystems)*. New York: Children's Press, 2000.

Stotksy, Sandra. *Rainforests: Tropical Treasures (Ranger Rick's Naturescope)*. Philadelphia, PA: Chelsea House Publishers, 1998.

Tangley, Laura. *The Rainforest (Earth at Risk)*. Philadelphia, PA: Chelsea House Publishers, 1992.

Taylor, Barbara. *In the Rainforest (Natural World Series)*. Hauppauge, NY: Barrons Juveniles, 1999.

Wood, Selina. *The Rainforest (Closer Look At)*. Brookfield, CT: Copper Beech Books, 1997.

Woods, Mae. *People of the Rain Forest*. Minneapolis, MN: Abdo Publishing Company, 1999.

Woods, Mae. *Plants of the Rain Forest*. Minneapolis, MN: Abdo Publishing Company, 1999.

Woods, Mae. *Protecting the Rain Forest*. Minneapolis, MN: Abdo Publishing Company, 1999.

Woods, Mae. *The Remarkable Rain Forest*. Minneapolis, MN: Abdo Publishing Company, 1999.

Wright-Frierson, Virginia. *A North American Rainforest Scrapbook*. New York: Walker & Company, 1999.

Organizations offering rain forest excursions

CET Foundation, International
201 West Main
Zeeland, MI 49464
(888) 748-9993
http://www.cetfoundation.org/

GORP travel
P.O. Box 1486
Boulder, CO 80306
(877) 440-GORP
http://gorptravel.gorp.com/

Journeys International, Inc.
107 Aprill Dr, Suite 3
Ann Arbor, MI 48103
(800) 255-8735
http://www.journeys-intl.com/specialty/family_travel.html

National Wildlife Federation Expeditions
11100 Wildlife Center Drive
Reston, VA 20190
(800) 606-9563
http://www.nwf.org/expeditions/for_families.html

Rascals in Paradise
2107 Van Ness Avenue, Suite 403
San Francisco, CA 94109
(415) 921-7000
http://www.rascalsinparadise.com/

Save The Rainforest
P.O. Box 16271
Las Cruces, NM 88004
(888) 608-9435
http://internet.cybermesa.com/~saverfn/

Thomson Family Adventures
14 Mount Auburn Street
Watertown, MA 02472
(800) 262-6255
http://www.familyadventures.com/

Voyagers International
P.O. Box 915
Ithaca, NY 14851
(800) 633-0299
http://www.voyagers.com/

Wildland Adventures
3516 NE 155th Street
Seattle, WA 98155
(800) 345-4453.
http://www.wildland.com/trips/specialtrips/family.asp

Museums, Zoos, and Parks

The Academy of Natural Sciences
1900 Benjamin Franklin Parkway
Philadelphia, PA 19103
(215) 299-1000
http://www.acnatsci.org
In the "African Hall," visitors can walk through a diorama of rain forests found at the equator.

American Museum of Natural History
Central Park West at 79th Street
New York, NY 10024
(212) 769-5100
http://www.amnh.org
Housed in the "Hall of Biodiversity" is a diorama of the Dzanga-Sangha rain forest of the Central African
Republic (C.A.R.).

Bronx Zoo/Wildlife Conservation Park
2300 Southern Boulevard
Bronx, NY 10460
(718) 367-1010
http://www.bronxzoo.org
Visitors can stroll an indoor rain forest where unique animals and plants live.

Cleveland Metroparks Zoo
3900 Wildlife Way
Cleveland, OH 44109
(216) 661-6500
http://www.clevelandzoo.com/
Explore two indoor acres of rain forest.

Columbia University's Biosphere 2 Center
32540 S. Biosphere Road
Oracle, AZ 85623
(520) 896-6400
http://www.bio2.edu
Biosphere 2 is a greenhouse located on three acres and containing several different biomes including a
    rain forest.

The Indianapolis Zoo
1200 W. Washington Street
Indianapolis, IN 46222
(317) 630-2001
http://www.indianapoliszoo.com
Visitors can roam a tropical rain forest biome and visit with the flora and fauna found there.

The Milwaukee Public Museum
800 West Wells Street
Milwaukee, WI 53233
(414) 278-2702
http://www.mpm.edu/default.asp
Offers a two-story exhibit that includes an elevated walkway through a simulated forest canopy, a
    waterfall, and a learning center with videos about tropical biology.

National Zoological Park
3001 Connecticut Avenue, N.W.
Washington, D.C. 20091
(202) 673-4717
http://natzoo.si.edu
Features an exhibit dedicated to the world's largest rain forest and the Amazon River.

San Diego Zoo
2920 Zoo Drive
San Diego CA 92101
(619) 234-3153
http://www.sandiegozoo.com/zoo/homepage.php3
"Gorilla Tropics" offers visitors a look at some African rain forest animals and plants.

Science Museum of Minnesota
120 W. Kellogg Boulevard.
St. Paul, MN 55102
(651) 221-9444
http://www.smm.org
Provides educational materials as well as a video entitled "Tropical Rainforest," which was originally
   shown in IMAX and OMNIMAX theaters.

University of Wisconsin Stevens Point Museum of Natural History
900 Reserve Street
Stevens Point, WI 54481
(715) 346-2858
http://www.uwsp.edu/museum/
Contains an ecosystem exhibit on tropical rain forests.

Zoo Atlanta
800 Cherokee Ave., SE
Atlanta, GA 30315
(404) 624-5600
http://www.zooatlanta.org/home.html
Exhibits its gorillas and some monkeys in an African rain forest setting.

Birds Index

anhingas **6**: 338
ant thrushes **2**: 59
antbirds **2**: 59; **3**: 162
antshrikes **10**: 595
argus pheasant **3**: 122
Asian fairy bluebird **7**: 397
Australian honeyeater
    4: *205*

barbets **4**: 206; **5**: 273, 276
bare-necked umbrella bird
    2: 99
bellbirds **2**: 61, 99
birds, general **1**: 43; **2**: **56–63**;
    6: 308, 337–338; **7**: 389,
    397, 400, 403–404, 410,
    412; **5**: 240; **9**: 536–538;
    10: 553, 558, 571, 584,
    594–595
birds of paradise **2**: 62–63,
    63, 83; **3**: 132
black-headed caiques **2**: *58*
boobies **7**: 363
bowerbirds **2**: 62; **3**: 132; **7**: 399
    satin **2**: *62*
broadbills **10**: 595

caracaras **10**: 554
cassowaries **1**: 27; **2**: 57, *57*;
    3: 122; **10**: 594
cave swiftlets **2**: 96
cockatoos **5**: 276
    Moluccan **8**: 433
    salmon-crested **8**: *432*
    slender-billed **8**: 433
cocks-of-the-rock **3**: 132
    4: 232
communication **3**: **121–123**
Congo peafowl **1**: 4
cormorants **7**: 363
courtship **2**: 61–62; **3**: **132–133**
crested honeycreepers
    10: 559
curassows **3**: 133

darters **4**: 207; **6**: 338
ducks **7**: 412

eagles **2**: 56, 60; **3**: **158–161**,
    163; **4**: 207; **7**: 403, 412;
    10: 594
    crowned **2**: 60; **3**: 158–161,
    158–159, 165; **7**: 403
    harpy **2**: 60, 79;
        3: 158–161, *161*; **4**: *232*
    Philippine, or
        monkey-eating **2**: 60;
        4: 177; **3**: 158–161, *160*;
        5: 282
egrets **7**: 363
endangered species
    4: **176–182**
Eungella honeyeater **1**: 27
exploitation **2**: 63
extinction **2**: 63; **4**: 202–203

feeding **4**: 205–207; **5**: 273–276
finches **2**: 58; **4**: 206; **5**: 273,
    276
flycatchers **2**: 58–59; **3**: 125;
    6: 308
food web **4**: **231–233**
frigates **7**: 363
fruit eaters **2**: 56–58

geese **7**: 412
grebes **6**: 338

hawks **2**: 60; **4**: 207; **7**: 403;
    10: 594
herbivores **3**: 166–167;
    5: **273–276**
herons **4**: 207; **7**: 412
honeyguides **8**: 436; **10**: 554
hornbills **1**: 4; **3**: 125; **4**: 178;
    10: 571
hummingbirds **2**: 56–57;
    4: 205, 221; **5**: 273, 275,
    286–287; **6**: 331, 337;

    7: 376, 404; **8**: 460, *460*,
    462, 478; **10**: 557, 591
    bee **5**: 286
    giant **5**: 286
    ruby-topaz **5**: 287
    saber-wing **2**: *56*
    stripe-tailed **5**: *287*
    violet-eared **5**: *286*

insect hunters **2**: 58–59

jacamars **10**: 595
jacanas **8**: 453
jewel thrushes **5**: 241

kingfishers **7**: 412
    Javan **6**: 303, *303*
kiwis **6**: 339, *339*; **7**: 406;
    10: 594

lories (SEE parrots)
lorikeets (SEE parrots)

macaws **2**: 56, 62–63; **4**: 206;
    5: 241, 276; **7**: 400;
    9: 518, 522; **10**: 571
    military **10**: *593*
    scarlet **4**: *233*
maleo **2**: 60, *60*; **4**: 179
manakins **10**: *594*, 595
megapodes **2**: 60

nectar eaters **2**: 56–57
nesting **2**: 60–63, 79, 96;
    7: 403–405
nightjars **7**: 410

oropendolas **7**: 403, 405;
    10: 554
    chestnut-headed **7**: *404*
ovenbirds **7**: 405
owls **2**: 56, 60; **4**: 207;
    7: 407–410, 412;
    8: **426–427**

Boldface numbers before colons indicate volumes; **boldface** numbers following colons indicate whole articles; *italic* numbers are the page numbers of illustrations.

owls (cont.)
    Australian masked 8: 426
    eagle 2: 60–61
    fishing 8: 427
    great gray 2: 60
    great horned 8: 426
    least pygmy 8: 426–427
    lesser sooty 8: 426
    Madagascar red 6: 349
    Papuan hawk 8: 427
    sooty 7: *409*; 8: 426
    spectacled 8: 427, *427*
    spotted 2: 61; 4: 182, *182*;
       10: 558
    Sumatran scops 6: 303
    tropical screech 8: *426*
    Verreux's eagle 2: 59

parrots 1: 4; 2: 58, *58*, 61–63;
    4: 203, 206; 5: 241, 276;
    7: 400; 8: **432–434**;
    10: 571
    African gray 3: 125; 8: 432
    Amazon 8: *433*
    cockatoos (SEE cockatoos)
    crimson rosella 7: 399
    eclectus 8: 432
    great-billed 8: 434
    king 8: 434
    lories 8: **432–434**
    lorikeets, rainbow 8: 434,
      434
    macaws (SEE macaws)
    palm parakeets 8: 433
    Puerto Rican 4: *203*
    red-sided 2: 61
pigeons 2: 57, 61; 3: 133; 5: 273
pittas 2: 59; 5: 241; 10: 595
    rainbow 7: 405
    Shneider's 6: 303
poaching 2: 63
pollination 2: 56–57, 64; 8: 462
puffbirds 6: 308

quetzals, resplendent 2: 61, *61*,
    99; 5: 251, *274*; 7: 400;
    8: 478; 10: 571
scarlet ibis 7: 363

scarlet minivet 7: 397
scrub turkeys 10: 551
scythebills 4: 207
seed eaters 2: 56–58
shrikes 4: 207
sunbirds 2: 56–57; 4: 205;
    5: 273; 7: 376; 10: 594
swallows 6: 308
swifts 6: 308; 7: 405
    Asian palm 7: 405

tailorbirds 7: 404
tanagers 10: 595
toucans 3: 123; 5: 273, 276;
    9: 518, 538, *538*;
    10: **566–567**, 594
    groove-billed toucanets
      10: *567*
    keel-billed 10: *566*
    toco 10: 552
tree creepers 10: 558
turacos 10: 595
tyrant flycatchers 7: 376

vultures 3: 141; 10: 596
    king *596*

warblers 2: 58; 6: 308; 7: 376
wild pine sergeants 2: 59
wood hoopoes 2: 59
wood ibises 7: 376
wood storks 7: 376
woodcreepers 2: 59
woodpeckers 2: 58–59, 61;
    4: 204, 207; 6: 309, 337;
    7: 389, 412; 10: 558, 571
    crimson-winged 2: *59*

yellow-green vireos 7: 376

Boldface numbers before colons indicate volumes; **boldface** numbers following colons indicate whole articles; *italic* numbers are the page numbers of illustrations.

Invertebrates Index

ants **1: 10–12**; **2:** 59, 85; **3:** 121, 123, 163; **4:** 184, 209, 217, 233; **5:** 241, 274; **6:** 305, 307, 310, 315; **7:** 415; **8:** 480; **10:** 560, 571, 584
army, or driver **1:** 10–11, *10;* **2:** *84;* **4:** 207, *231;* **5:** 241
leaf-cutter **1:** 11, *11;* **3:** 162; **5:** 252–253; **10:** *553,* 554
legionary **1:** 11
weaver **1:** 12, *12;* **7:** 405
aphids **5:** 274; **6:** 307

bees **1: 34–36**; **4:** 205; **7:** 403; **8:** 461–462
carpenter **1:** 35, *35;* **8:** 461
euglossine **4:** 222
honey **1:** 35; **8:** *461*
stingless **1:** 35
bees and wasps **1: 34–36**; **5:** 275–276; **6:** 305, 308, 310, 313, 315, 331 (SEE ALSO wasps)
beetles **1: 37–41**, 46–47; **3:** 141, 163; **5:** 240–241, 273, 275; **6:** 305, 310–311, 313; **10:** 554, 572, 584
bombardier **6:** 306
carrion **3:** 141; **6:** 314
chafer, Australian **1:** *39*
click **1:** *37,* 47
dung **3:** 141; **5:** 241, *241;* **6:** 307, 314
fiddle, or violin **1:** 39
fireflies **1:** 41, 46–47; **3:** 133
fungus **6:** 313
glowworms **1:** 46, *46*
goliath **1:** 40
harlequin **4:** *232;* **6:** 307
hercules **1:** 40
jewel **1:** 41
long-horned **1:** 38
harlequin **1:** 38
rhinoceros **1:** 40–41
three-horned **1:** *40*
stag **1:** 39
tortoise **1:** *38, 41*
water **6:** 339
bugs **2: 65–68**; **4:** 205; **6:** 310–311, 313, 315
anatomy **2:** 65–68
aquatic **2:** 65–67
assassin **2:** 68
African **2:** 68, *68*
backswimmers **2:** 66
defense **2:** 66
feeding **4:** 205
giant water bugs **2:** 67, *67*
life cycle **2:** 65–66
peanut **7:** *401,* 402
rhodnius **2:** 68
shield **6:** 315, *315*
stinkbugs **2:** 66
water boatmen **2:** *65,* 66
water scorpions **2:** 66–67, *66*
water stick insects **2:** 67
water striders **2:** 68
butterflies **1:** 7; **3:** 123; **9:** 536–538; **10:** 557–558, 591
bird wings **2:** 70, *70*
Queen Alexandra's **2:** 70, *70;* **6:** 310
bluebottle swallowtails **2:** *71*
glass-wings **2:** 71
heliconiids **2:** *69,* 70; **4:** *232;* **6:** 306–307; **8:** 452
Isabella tiger **6:** 315
leaf **2:** 71
Madagascan red-and-gold skipper **4:** *177*
morphos **2:** 72, *72;* **6:** 304
blue morpho **10:** 552
nymphalids **6:** 306
owl **2:** 73
Phyciodes philyra **6:** 315 (SEE ALSO butterflies and moths)
butterflies and moths **2: 69–73**; **4:** 205; **5:** 275; **6:** 304–307, *304,* 310, *311,* 313, 315, 330–331; **8:** 461
defenses **2:** 71–75
life cycle **2:** 69–70, 79
poisonous **2:** 69–70, 72
puddling **2:** 71, *71*
species of moths (SEE moths)

caterpillars **3:** 121; **4:** 204, 207; **5:** 274, *275;* **6:** 311, 313, 315
centipedes **2: 97**; **4:** 207, 217; **5:** 241; **6:** 315; **10:** 572
scolopendra **2:** 97, *97*
cicadas **2: 106**, *106;* **3:** 121–122, 133; **6:** 304, *308*
cockroaches **2:** 96; **3: 120**; **4:** 233; **5:** 240; **7:** 407, 409
giant tropical **3:** 120
Madagascan hissing **3:** *120*
wood roaches **3:** 120
communication **3: 121–123**
copepod **3:** 138, *138*
courtship **3: 132–133**
crabs **3:** 138–139, 141, 163; **10:** 599
coconut **3:** 138; **5:** 273
hermit **3:** 138
land **4:** 233
Caribbean land **3:** 139
red land **3:** *139*
robber **6:** *313*

Boldface numbers before colons indicate volumes; **boldface** numbers following colons indicate whole articles; *italic* numbers are the page numbers of illustrations.

crickets **3**: 121–122, *121;*
  5: 267–270; **7**: 408
  brachytrupes membranaceus
    5: 269
  bush **2**: 75
  cave **2**: 75
  rhicnogryllus lepidus **5**: 269
  wetas **7**: 406
  (SEE ALSO grasshoppers,
    crickets, and katydids)
crustaceans **3**: **138–139**; **6**: 310,
    314
  crabs (SEE crabs)
  prawns **7**: 363
  shrimps **3**: 138
  wood lice **3**: 138–139

dragonflies and damselflies
    3: **154–155**; **6**: 305, *305;*
    10: 599
  aeshnid **3**: 154
  giant damselfly **3**: 155, *155*

endangered species **4**: 176, 181

fireflies (SEE beetles)
fleas **6**: 304, 336
flies **3**: 141; **4**: **223–224**, 233;
    6: 307; **8**: 461, 473
  botflies **4**: 223–224
  fungus **6**: 313
  New Zealand glowworm, or
    fungus gnat **1**: 47;
    4: 224, *224*
  pantophthalmid **4**: 223;
    6: 307, 313
  robber **4**: 224; **6**: *306*, 307
  tsetse **4**: 223, *223*
food web **4**: **231–233**

grasshoppers **3**: 122; **4**: 204;
    6: 307, 313
  chlorotypus **5**: 268
  proscopia **5**: 268
  short-winged **5**: *268*
  zonoceros **5**: 269
  (SEE ALSO grasshoppers,
    crickets, and katydids)

grasshoppers, crickets, and
    katydids **5**: **267–270**;
    6: 305
  crickets (SEE crickets)
  grasshoppers (SEE
    grasshoppers)
  katydids (SEE katydids)

herbivores **3**: 166–167;
    5: **273–276**

insects **6**: **304–307**, 310,
    338–339; **9**: 526; **10**: 581,
    583–584 (for species, see
    individual entries)
invertebrates, general
    6: **310–315**; **7**: 410 (for
    species, see individual
    entries)

katydids **2**: 75; **4**: 204;
    5: 267–270, *267, 270;*
    6: 313, 315
  lichen **5**: 269, *269*
  mimetica incisa **5**: 270
  zabalius apicalis **5**: 270
  (SEE ALSO grasshoppers,
    crickets, and katydids)

leeches **4**: 205–206; **6**: 310, 312,
    325, *325*, 336–337; **7**: 389;
    10: 598, 603

mantises **2**: 75; **3**: 133, *133;*
    4: 207; **6**: 308, 311, 315;
    7: **364–365**, *364–365*
  Archimantis **7**: 364
  Asian flower **2**: 75
millipedes **3**: 140–141; **4**: 217;
    5: 240; **6**: 310–311, 314;
    7: **377**, *377;* **10**: 572
  giant pill **3**: *140*
mollusks **6**: 312
mosquitoes **2**: 64, 89;
    3: 121–122, 150–151, *150;*
    5: 275, 291; **6**: 304,
    306–307, 311; **7**: 381, **391**,
    391; **8**: 430; **10**: 599

moths **2**: **69–73**; **4**: 205; **5**: 275;
    6: 304–305, *307*,
    307–308, 313, 315;
    7: 410; **8**: 460–461
  hawk moths **6**: 307;
    8: 424
  silk moths **2**: 69, 72–73;
    6: 307, *307*
  uraniids **2**: 73, *73*
  (SEE ALSO butterflies and
    moths)

prawns (SEE crustaceans)
praying mantises
    (SEE mantises)

scorpions **2**: 79; **5**: 241; **9**: **514**,
    514
slugs **4**: 233 (SEE ALSO slugs
    and snails)
  Veronicella **9**: 529
slugs and snails **6**: 310–312;
    9: **528–529**, *528–529*
snails **2**: 64; **4**: 217, 233; **5**: 240;
    7: 410; **10**: 572
  Achatina fulica **9**: 528–529
  Papustyla **9**: 529
  (SEE ALSO slugs and
    snails)
spiders **2**: 74–75, 79, 89;
    3: 122; **4**: 205, 217;
    5: 241; **6**: 308–310,
    315; **7**: 408–409;
    9: **539–543**;
    10: 572, 581
  bolas **9**: 541
  crab **6**: *308*; **9**: 542–543,
    542
  Curimagua **9**: 539
  gladiator **9**: 543
  goliath bird-eating
    tarantulas **6**: 310; **9**: 539,
    541, *543*
  jumping **9**: 542–543
    orsima ichneumon
    9: 542
  net-casting **7**: *410*
  nursery web **6**: 315

Boldface numbers before colons indicate volumes; **boldface** numbers following colons indicate whole articles; *italic* numbers are the page numbers of illustrations.

orb web **9**: 540

    Gasteracantha **9**: 540

    golden orb web **9**: *540*

    Nephila **9** : 540

red kite **9**: *539*

trap-door **9**: 542

    Liphistius, giant trap-door
      9: *541*, 542

wolf **9**: 543

termites **1**: 28; **3**: 140, 163;
    4: 204, *232*; **5**: 240, 274;
    6: 305, 307, 313;
    7: 403–404; **10**: 553–554,
    560–561, *560–561*, 571,
    582

    Macrotermes **10**: *560, 561*

thrips **4**: 221

wasps **1**: 34–36; **7**: *403*, 405;
    10: 554, 581, 591

    paper **7**: 403

    potter **7**: 403

    tiger hornet **1**: 36

    yellow jackets **1**: 36

    Zethus **1**: 36

    (SEE ALSO bees and wasps)

weevils, toothpick **10**: 552

whip scorpions **2**: 96; **5**: 241

worms **3**: 140, 151; **4**: 217, 233;
    6: 310, 312–313,
    336–337; **10**: 572,
    598–599, **602–603**,
    602–603

    velvet **2**: 99; **6**: 312, *312*,
    315; **10**: 603

Boldface numbers before colons indicate volumes; **boldface** numbers following colons indicate whole articles; *italic* numbers are the page numbers of illustrations.

Mammals Index

agoutis 4: 206, 232; 5: 240;
  6: *331*
anoas 6: 302–303
anteaters 1: **13**; 4: 207;
    6: 308–309; 7: 407;
    9: 518; 10: 571
  giant 1: 13
  kinkajou 4: 207
  spiny, or echidna 6: 353
  tree, or tamandua 1: 13,
    13; 4: 207
  two-toed, or silky 1: 13;
    4: *232*; 6: 309, *309*
antelopes 1: **14–15**
  bongo 1: *14*, 15
  duikers 1: 15
  nilgai 7: 390
  pygmy 1: 15
  royal 1: 15
  suni 3: 160
apes 1: **16–18**; 6: 356; 8: 469
armadillos 1: **19**; 4: 207; 6: 309;
    7: 407
  giant 1:19
  lesser fairy, or pink fairy
    1: 19
  nine-banded 1: 19, *19*
aye-ayes 1: 4; 4: 206, *206*;
    6: 348–349, 354; 7: 408

babirusas 4: 179, 8: *445*, 446
baboons 3: 123
bandicoots 1: 27
bats 1: **29–32**; 2: 78–79, 84, 96,
    100; 4: 177, 207,
    221–222; 5: 275–276;
    6: 308, 352, 354; 7: 363,
    407, 409; 8: 462; 10: 595
  bulldog, or fishing 1: *30*
  false vampire 1: 30; 2: 100
  fringe-lipped 1: 31
  fruit 1: 4; 9: 518; 10: 551
  Kitti's hog-nosed 1: 30;
    6: 352

leaf-nosed 6: *352*
long-nosed 8: *462*
Queensland tube-nosed
    1: *32*
short-tailed fruit 1: 32
vampire 1: 30; 2: 100;
    4: 205
  common 1: 30–31
  hairy-legged 1: 30
  white-winged 1: 30–31
white tent-building 1: *31*,
    32; 2: 78
bears 1: 33; 2: 87; 4: 232;
    5: 276; 6: 355; 9: 516
  black 1: 33; 7: 397, 413;
    10: 558, *558*
  grizzly 1: 33
  sloth 1: 33, *33*
  spectacled 1: 33; 2: 87
  sun 1: 33; 2: *85*, 87
beavers 7: 399
bush babies (SEE Galagos)
bushdogs 2: 86, *86*

capybaras 4: *232*; 5: 275; 6: 339,
    353, 355; 9: 503–506, *504*,
    536–537
carnivores 2: **84–87**; 3: 167
cats 2: 85–86, **90–93**, 100;
    3: 123, 133; 6: 356;
    7: 409–410; 9: 518;
    10: 595
  African golden 2: 93
  fishing 2: *90*, 93
  flat-headed 2: 93
  iriomote 2: 92
  jaguars (SEE jaguars)
  jaguarundis (SEE
    jaguarundis)
  leopards (SEE leopards)
  marbled 2: 93
  margays 2: 93, *93*, 100
  ocelots 2: 93, 100
  tigers (SEE tigers)

chevrotains 5: *275*
  water 1: 5
chimpanzees 1: 2, 4, 16–17, *17*;
    2: **103–105**; 3: 125, 129,
    165; 4: 193, 231; 6: 337;
    7: 399, 405
  bonobo 1: 17, 45;
    2: 103–105, *104*
  common 2: *103*
civets 2: 87, **107**
  palm 2: 87, *107*
coatis 2: 87, 100; 3: 165; 6: 355,
    355
communication 3: **121–123**
cougar, or mountain lion
    7: **412–413**
courtship 3: **132–133**
cuscuses 6: 301

deer 1: 25, 28; 2: 75; 3: 123,
    142–145; 4: 204–205;
    5: 273; 6: 302, 355–356;
    7: 363, 407–408; 9: 526;
    10: 553
  axis, or chital 1: 25; 3: 143,
    143; 7: 363
  black-tailed 7: 413
  lesser mouse 6: 302
  muntjac 3: 142, 145, *145*
  red brocket 3: 144–145,
    144
  rusas 6: 302
  sambar 1: 25; 3: *142*, 145;
    7: 390; 9: *517*
  spotted 7: 390
  Visayan spotted 3: 145
dolphins, river 3: **152**; 4: 232;
    9: 502, 518; 10: 595
  botos 3: 152, *152*
  susus 3: 152
drills 4: 181
dugongs, or manatees (SEE
  manatees)

Boldface numbers before colons indicate volumes; **boldface** numbers following colons indicate whole articles; *italic* numbers are the page numbers of illustrations.

elephants **3:** **169;** **4:** 204; **5:** 274,
6: 352, 355; **10:** 583
African **3:** 125, 129, 169;
4: 201; **6:** 331
Asian **1:** 25; **3:** 169, *169;*
5: 274; **6:** 303; **7:** 390,
397; **10:** *568*
elk **7:** 399, 413, **10:** 558
Roosevelt elk **7:** *413*
endangered species **4: 176–182**

food web **4: 231–233**
foxes **4:** 232; **7:** 409
gray **2:** 86

galagos **3:** 123; **5:** 254, *254,*
274; **7:** 408; **8:** 468
gaurs **4:** *176;* **7:** 390
genets **6:** 354, *354*
giant otters **4:** 181; **5:** 257, *257*
gibbons **1:** 17–18; **3:** *117;*
5: **258–259,** *259;* **6:** 337;
8: *470*
hoolock **10:** 551
Kloss's **5:** 259
siamang **1:** 18, *18;* **5:** 258,
258
gorillas **1:** 4, 16–17; **3:** 124, 129;
4: 193; **5: 264–266;**
6: 356; **7:** 405; **8:** 458
eastern lowland **3:** 125,
125; **5:** 264, *265*
mountain **1:** 16, 45; **4:** 182;
5: 264, *264;* **7:** *405*
western lowland **1:** *16;*
5: 264; **7:** 399

herbivores **3:** 166–167;
5: 273–276
hippopotamuses, pygmy **1:** 4
hogs **2:** 75; **4:** 233; **5:** 276
honey possums (SEE possums)

indris (SEE lemurs)

jaguars **2:** 85, 86, 90–91, *91,* 92,
100; **4:** *232–233;* **6: 316,**
316; **7:** 408;

jaguarundis **2:** 86, *92, 93*

kangaroos
muskrat **1:** 27
tree **10:** **578–579,** *578–579*

lemurs **1:** 4, 42; **4:** 182, 190;
6: **326–327,** 348–349;
8: 455, 468, *468;* **10:** 595
aye-ayes (SEE aye-ayes)
black **6:** *326, 327*
brown **1:** 42
gentle **6:** 327, *327*
golden bamboo **4:** 176
indris **1:** 4, 42; **3:** 147;
6: **326–327,** 348; **4:** 182
red-bellied **1:** *43*
red-fronted **1:** *43*
red-ruffed **6:** 349, *349*
rufous mouse **8:** 468–469
sifakas **3:** 163; **6:** 327, *337*
diademed **1:** *42;* **4:** 182
sportive **6:** 327
leopards **1:** 25; **2:** 90–92; **3:** 133;
7: 363, 390, 408
clouded **2:** 93; **8:** *457*
lorises **6:** 346; **7:** 408;
8: 468
slender **6:** *346*
slow **7:** *408*

mammals, general **4:** 203–204,
206; **6:** 336, **352–356;**
7: 410; **10:** 595
manatees **6: 357,** *357;* **9:** 502,
518; **10:** 595
Amazonian **4:** 181
marmosets and tamarins **5:** 274;
7: 366–367, 387; **8:** 469
buffy-headed marmoset
4: 180–181; **9:** 536
common marmosets **7:** 366
emperor tamarin **7:** 367,
367
golden lion tamarin **4:** 180,
180; **7:** 367; **9:** 536
pygmy marmoset **7:** *366*
saddle-back tamarin **7:** 367

marsupials **6:** 301, 309, 338,
353–354; **10:** 595
mice (SEE rodents)
mink **7:** 412
mongooses **7:** 384, 409; **10:** 551
crab-eating **7:** 384
ring-tailed **7:** 384, *384*
stripe-necked **7:** 384
monkeys **2:** 77, 79, 100; **3:** 116,
121–123, 133; **4:** 181,
201, 204, 221, 232;
5: 273, 276; **6:** 353,
355–356; **7: 385–388;**
8: 469; **9:** 518, 536, 538;
10: 552, 571, 584
capuchins **4:** *232;* **7:** 385
colobus **3:** 165; **7:** 385–386
black **7:** 387
black-and-white **7:** 398
Kenyan **7:** *388*
red **1:** *4;* **5:** *273;* **7:** 387
398,
DeBrazza's **7:** 385
douroucouli, or night
monkey **7:** 388, *407,* 408
guenons **7:** 386–387
howler **2:** 79; **3:** 123, *123;*
7: 386–387
langur **1:** 25; **3:** 143, *143;*
7: 386
douc langur **7:** *385*
leaf **1:** 25; **7:** 386
macaque **1:** 25; **6:** 302;
7: 386
black **4:** 177
bonnet **7:** 390
lion-tailed **1:** 25
long-tailed **6:** 301
pig-tailed **1:** 25; **7:** 385
stump-tailed **7:** 390
toque **1:** 25
mandrills **7:** 386–387, *387*
mangabeys **7:** 386–387
marmosets (SEE
marmosets and tamarins)
muriqui **4:** 180–181; **9:** 536
proboscis **6:** *301,* 302;
7: 386, *386*

Boldface numbers before colons indicate volumes; **boldface** numbers following colons indicate whole articles; *italic* numbers are the page numbers of illustrations.

monkeys (cont.)
  rhesus 7: 388
  spider 2: 79, *79*; 7: 385
  spot-nosed 8: *459*
  squirrel 4: *204*; 7: 387;
    8: *469*
  tamarins (SEE marmosets
    and tamarins)
  Thomas's leaf 6: 302
  titi 7: 387
  uakaris 7: 387

numbats 4: 207

okapis 1: 28, 45; 3: 125; 4: 205;
  6: 355; 7: *418*, *418*
opossums (SEE possums and
  opossums)
orangutans 1: 16–18; 3: 163;
  4: *177*, *178*; 6: 302–303;
  7: 405, **419**, *419*
otters 7: 399, 412; 9: 502;
  10: 595
  giant otters (SEE giant
    otters)

pademelons, red-necked
  10: 551, *551*
pangolins 4: 207; 10: 571
peccaries 2: 75, 100; 3: 165;
  4: 232; 6: 355–356
  (SEE ALSO pigs and
  peccaries)
pigs and peccaries 5: 276;
    8: **445–446**; 9: 526
  babirusas (SEE babirusas)
  bearded pigs 7: 376, *376*;
    8: 445
  collared peccaries 8: 446
  giant forest hogs 8: 446,
    446
  red river hogs 8: *458*
  white-lipped peccaries
    8: 446
  (SEE ALSO peccaries)
porcupines (SEE rodents)
porpoises 10: 595
possums and opossums 6: 353,

  355; 7: 399, 408;
    8: **466–467**
gliding possums 8: 467,
  467
honey possums 3: 163;
  4: 205; 5: 273, *276*;
  6: 353
lutrine opossums 8: 467
mouse opossums 6: *353*
pygmy possums 8: 466
ring-tailed possums 8: 467
spotted cuscuses 8: *466*,
  467
water opossums 8: 467
primates 1: 7, 25, 45; 7: 398,
  400, 405; 8: **468–470**,
  468–470; 10: 552, 557, 595
  (for species, see individual
  entries)
puma 2: 90–91

quolls, spotted tail 7: 408

rabbits 1: 28; 10: 553
raccoons 10: 571
red pandas 8: **481**, *481*
rhinoceroses 1: 25; 5: 274;
  6: 302–303; 9: 498;
  10: 551, 583
  Javan 4: 178; 6: 302; 9: 498
  Sumatran 4: 178–179, *178*;
    6: 302; 9: **498**, *498*
rodents 9: **503–506**, 536;
  10: 548–549, 558
  agoutis 9: 503–504, 536
  capybaras (SEE capybaras)
  guinea pigs 9: 504, 506
  mice 7: 408; 9: 504–506
    pencil-tailed tree 9: 505
  pacas 9: *503*, 504, 536
  porcupines 9: 503–506
    tree porcupine, or
    coendou 9: *506*
  rats 9: 504–506
    naked-tailed climbing
    9: *505*
  swamp 9: 505
  water 9: 505

shrews 6: 308–309; 7: 410
  tree shrews 3: 123, 133,
    6: *356*
  squirrels (SEE squirrels)
  voles, red-backed 7: 412

shrews (SEE rodents)
sifakas (SEE lemurs)
sloths 2: 79, 100; 3: 163; 6: 354,
  356; 9: **527**, *527*; 10: 554,
  554
squirrels 5: 273; 6: 337, 354;
  7: 390, 403, 412;
  9: 503–506;
  10: **548–549**, 551, 571
  Douglas 10: *548*
  flying 1: 25; 6: 338; 7: 399;
    9: 505, 516; 10: 549,
    558, 595
    northern 7: 412, *412*
  Malabar 7: 397
  marmots 10: 548, *549*
  pygmy 10: 548
  scaly-tailed 10: 549
    African scaly-tailed
    9: 505

tamarins (SEE marmosets and
  tamarins)
tapirs 2: 100; 3: 165; 4: 179,
  204; 5: 274, 275; 7: 398;
  10: 553, **555**, *555*, 583
tarsiers 6: 302, *302*; 8: 468–469
tenrecs 4: 207; 10: 595
tigers 1: 25, *25*; 2: 84, 86,
  90–92; 3: 133; 6: 302–303;
  7: 363, 390, 397, 408–409;
  10: **562–563**, *562–563*
tree kangaroos (SEE kangaroos)

voles (SEE rodents)

Boldface numbers before colons indicate volumes; **boldface** numbers following colons indicate whole articles; *italic* numbers are the page numbers of illustrations.

Peoples Index

Achuar people 9: 538
Aka people 1: 3; 3: 129; 5: 288
Akha people 5: 277
Arara people 8: 435
Ashaninka people 1: **20–21**, *20–21*
Asmat people 5: 289, *289*; 6: 343

Baka people 3: 125; 5: 279; 8: 437, *437*; 9: 517
Bantu people 1: 3

caboclos 4: 215, *215*
Chiricoa people 5: 289; 7: 376

Dyak people 3: **156–157**, *156–157*; 4: *197*; 5: 280, 288–289; 8: *442*; 9: 495

Efe people 3: 125

fishing 4: **215–216**

Guahibo people 5: 289; 7: 376

homes 5: **277–281**, 293
Huaorani people 7: 417
hunter-gatherers 3: 125, 129; 5: 278–279, 283, **288–289**; 8: 435–437, 458

Iban people 3: 156; 4: *196*; 9: 497
Ibo people 5: **292–293**, *292–293*

Kaluli people 6: **317–318**; 8: 441
Kayapo people 4: 196; 6: **319–320**, *319–320*
Kuna people 6: **321–322**, *321–322*; 7: 396

Machiguenga people 9: 495

Makah people 6: **350–351**, *350–351*
Maya people 2: 61; 7: **368–369**, *368–369*; 9: 526
Mbuti people 1: 3, *3*; 3: 125, 149; 5: 279, *279*, 288; 7: **370–371**, *370–371*; 8: **436–437**, *436*
Mende people 4: 216
Miskito people 7: **382–383**, *382–383*; 9: *496*

Panara people 9: 496
Penan people (SEE Punan)
people of the rain forest 8: **435–442**
Piaroa people 4: *195*; 5: 281, *281*; 8: **438–439**, *439–440*
Punan, or Penan people 8: 436–437, 480

Quinault people 8: **471–472**, *471–472*

resettlement 2: 94–95; 6: 319; 9: **494–497**

Semang people 5: 289; 8: 436

Tikuna people 4: 215–216; 8: 440
Tlingit people 10: **564–565**, *564–565*
Twa people 1: 3; 3: 125

U'wa people 7: 417

Warrau people 5: 289; 8: *440*

Yanomami people 3: 149, 151; 5: 280; 8: **438–440**; 10: **604–605**, *604–605*
Yoruba people 5: 279–280, 292

Boldface numbers before colons indicate volumes; **boldface** numbers following colons indicate whole articles; *italic* numbers are the page numbers of illustrations.

Places Index

Africa **1**: **2–5**, *2*, 44–45; **3**: 114, 124–125, 129, 141, 146; **4**: 181, 189–190, 193, 196

Alaska **10**: 556, 564, 569

Amazon rain forest **2**: 94–95, 108–9; **3**: 128; **10**: 593

Amazon River **1**: 6–7, 20; **5**: 290–291; **9**: *499*, 501–502, 499, 518, 522, 537; **10**: 597, 600, 604

Amazon River basin **3**: 115, 146; **4**: 192, 217–218; **6**: 344; **7**: 376, 378, 380–381, 416; **9**: 496–497, 499, 501; **10**: 581, 598, 600

Amazonia **1**: 2, **6–7**, *6*, 44; **4**: 80, 189, 195, 215; **6**: 301; **8**: 476–477; **9**: 489, 494–495, 497, 518, 535–538

Angel Falls (SEE Cherun-Meru)

Angkor Wat **5**: 278

Argentina **4**: 180; **9**: 535; **10**: 550, 552

Ariau River **1**: 6

Asia **1**: **22–25**, 44; **3**: 114

Australia **1**: 6, **26–27**, *26*; **3**: 115; **4**: 189–190, 201; **9**: 487; **10**: 550–552, 581

Belize **2**: 98–99; **3**: 129; **10**: 569

Bohorok River gorge **6**: *300*

Bolivia **3**: 146

Borneo **1**: 23, *23*, 43; **3**: 156–157; **4**: 177–178, 196; **6**: 300–301, *343*; **7**: 376; **9**: 495, 497

Brahmaputra River **4**: 217

Brazil **1**: 6, 44; **2**: 94–95, 109; **3**: 146–147, 151; **4**: 180, 195–196; **5**: 291; **6**: 344; **9**: 535–536, 538; **10**: 550, 552, 604–605

Burma (SEE Myanmar)

Cambodia **4**: 189; **6**: 343

Cameroon **1**: 3, 5; **6**: 343; **9**: 517; **10**: 581

Canada **9**: 515; **10**: 556

canopy **2**: 56, 61, 66, 71, **76–79**, *76–77*, 78, 100; **3**: 116–117, 124, 129, 153, 165, 167, 170–171; **4**: 198–200; **8**: 450, 477; **10**: 551–552, 570–572, 583–584, 597–598

Caroni swamp, Trinidad **7**: 363

caves **2**: 96

Central African Republic **1**: 3, 5; **3**: 129

Central America **1**: 43–44; **2**: 63, 94, **98–101**, 98; **4**: 179–180, 189; **9**: 487, 536; **10**: 581

Cherun-Meru, or Angel Falls **4**: 199

Chile **9**: 515, 535; **10**: 556

China **1**: 22; **10**: 550, 558

cloud forests **1**: 2; **2**: 99

Colombia **2**: 94, 99; **3**: 146; **7**: 417; **9**: 534–536

Congo **3**: **124–125**, 146; **4**: 181, 199

Congo, Democratic Republic of the **1**: 3, 5; **6**: 343

Congo Republic **1**: 3

Congo River **7**: 370; **9**: 501–502, *502*

Congo River basin **1**: 3–5, 45; **10**: 581

Costa Rica **1**: 44; **2**: 94, 98–99, 98; **3**: 129; **10**: 568

Ecuador **2**: 101; **3**: 146; **9**: 488, 535, 537–538

Equatorial Guinea **1**: 3

Fiji **4**: 189

forest floor **2**: 76–77, 99–100;

3: 165; **5**: **240–241**, *240*, 244, 253; **9**: 523–524; **10**: 572

French Guiana **4**: *200*

Gabon **1**: 3; **6**: 343

Guatemala **2**: 94, 98–99; **4**: 218

Guinea **10**: 581

Guyana **8**: *477*

Halmahera **6**: 300

Hawaii **10**: 558–559, *559*

Hoh rain forest **8**: *475*

Honduras **2**: 94, 98–99

igapo forest **1**: *6*, 7; **4**: 218; **10**: *570*, 585

Iguaçu Falls **9**: 535; **10**: 552, *552*

India **1**: 22; **4**: 195, 217; **6**: 342; **7**: 389; **10**: 551, 581

Indochina **4**: 189

Indonesia **1**: 22–23, 45; **2**: 95; **4**: 177, 189, 195; **5**: 238; **6**: **300–303**, 343–344; **7**: 416; **9**: 495, *497*; **10**: 569, 581

Indus River **4**: 217

Ituri forest **7**: 370, **10**: 581

Ivory Coast **3**: 146; **10**: 581, 599

Japan **10**: 558

Jatun Sacha Biological Station **9**: 488, 537

Java **6**: 300–301

Kapawi Lodge and Ecological Reserve **9**: 538

Kenyir, Lake **10**: 569

Kinabalu, Mount **1**: 23, *23*, 46

Korea **10**: 558

Laos **1**: 22; **4**: 189

Boldface numbers before colons indicate volumes; **boldface** numbers following colons indicate whole articles; *italic* numbers are the page numbers of illustrations.

Madagascar **1**: 3–4, 42–43, 45;
    2: 102; **3**: 146–147; **4**: 182,
    185, 190; **6**: 347–349,
    347–348; **8**: 455; **9**: 526,
    526; **10**: 550, 581
Malaysia **1**: 23; **3**: *147*; **4**: 189,
    195; **6**: 343; **9**: 496–497
mangrove forest **7**: **362–363**,
    362, 394; **9**: 508–510, *510*,
    522, *522*; **10**: 575
Mexico **2**: 99; **3**: 146; **4**: 180
monsoon forest **1**: 22–23, 25;
    7: **389–390**, *389*; **9**: 499,
    517, 518; **10**: 551
Monte Azules Biosphere Reserve
    7: 369
Monteverde cloud forest **8**: *478*
Mount Kinabalu **1**: 23, *23*, 46
Myanmar **1**: 22; **4**: 189; **6**: 343;
    10: 550

national parks **1**: 2; **3**: 125–126,
    128–129; **6**: 303;
    7: 389–390, **395–400**;
    9: 496; **10**: 551, 559
  Bwindi Impenetrable Forest
    7: *399*; **8**: *452*
  Chitwan **7**: 395, 397
  Cross River **7**: 399
  Dzanga-Ndoki **3**: 129
  Eungella **1**: 27
  Gombe Stream **1**: 2
  Guatopo **7**: 397
  Gunung Leuser **6**: 303
  Kahuzi-Biega **3**: 125
  Kerinci Sablat **6**: 303;
    7: 397
  Khao Yai **7**: *395*, 397
  Korup **7**: 395, 398–399
  Kuna Indian Forest Park
    7: 396
  La Amistad **7**: 400
  Lamington **7**: 399
  Manú **4**: 194; **7**: 399–400,
    400
  Masaola **6**: 349
  Olympic **7**: *392*, 399, 413;
    9: *507*

Periyar **7**: 389, *389*, 397
Ranomafana **7**: 396, *396*
Taman Negara **7**: 397, *397*
Tamborine **1**: *26*
Ujung Kulon **6**: 303; **9**: 498
Xingu **6**: 319; **9**: 496
Yasuni **7**: 417
Nepal **1**: 22
New Guinea **4**: 190; **6**: 300;
    7: 416; **10**: 581
New Zealand **7**: **406**, *406*;
    8: 476; **10**: 556
Nicaragua **2**: 98–99
Nigeria **1**: 3; **3**: 146; **4**: 195;
    6: 342
North America **2**: 90;
    7: **411–413**, *411*;
    10: 556–559

Olympic National Park (SEE
    national parks)
Orinoco River **7**: 376, 417;
    10: 604
Orinoco River basin **4**: 217–218

Pacific islands **10**: 556, 558, 581
Panama **1**: 43; **2**: 98–99
Panama Canal **7**: 391; **10**: 599
Papua New Guinea **4**: 189
Paraguay **2**: 108; **9**: 535;
    10: 550, *550*, 552
Peru **1**: 6, 20–21, 43–44; **4**: 194;
    7: 417
Philippines **1**: 22–23; **2**: 64,
    108; **3**: 146; **4**: 177, 189,
    195, 216; **7**: 416; **9**: 496

Queensland **1**: 26–27
Quinault rain forest **8**: 471–472,
    471

rain forests **8**: **474–478**
  structure **8**: 474, *474*
  types of **8**: 475–478
rivers **3**: 130, 152; **9**: **499–502**,
    499–500, 518; **10**: 598–601
Rondônia **1**: *7*; **4**: 180
Rwanda **4**: 201

Sepilok Rehabilitation Center
    4: *177, 178*
Sierra Leone **1**: 3; **4**: 216
South America **1**: 44; **2**: 94;
    4: 179–180, 189–190, 215,
    217; **9**: 496, **534–538**;
    10: 552, 581
Southeast Asia **3**: 146, 148;
    4: 177
Sri Lanka **10**: 581
subtropical rain forests **9**: 517,
    535; **10**: **550–552**, 573
Sulawesi **4**: 179; **6**: 300–302
Sumatra **4**: 178; **6**: 300–301,
    303; **9**: *525*

Taiwan **10**: 550
Tanzania **1**: 2
temperate rain forests **2**: 53, 60,
    90, 108–109; **3**: 114–115,
    165; **7**: 411–413;
    9: 515–516, 535;
    10: 548–549, **556–559**,
    564–566, 569
Thailand **1**: 22–23; **3**: 146;
    4: 188–189; **6**: 342–343;
    9: 496
tierra firme forest **1**: 6
tropical rain forest **10**: **580–585**,
    580, 582
  lowland **10**: 580

Uganda **1**: 3
understory **2**: 76, 100; **10**: 571,
    585, **590–591**
United Nations **9**: 487
United States **3**: 115

varzea forest **1**: 7
Venezuela **4**: 195, 199;
    10: 604–605
Vietnam **1**: 22; **4**: 189

Wallace's line **6**: 300
Wanariset Research Institute for
    Sustainable Forestry **9**: *487*
West Indies **10**: 581

Boldface numbers before colons indicate volumes; **boldface** numbers following colons indicate whole articles; *italic* numbers are the page numbers of illustrations.

Xingu National Park (SEE
    national parks)

Boldface numbers before colons indicate volumes; **boldface** numbers following colons indicate whole articles; *italic* numbers are the page numbers of illustrations.

Plants, Algae, and Microorganisms Index

acacia 8: 461
alamendro 4: 220
alerce 9: 516
algae 4: 217; 5: 252, 291;
    8: 451; 10: 553
annatto 9: 519
anthuriums 10: 591
Aphelandra 9: *523*
aroids 10: 581
arums 4: 219–220
    titan 4: 222
    white arum lilies 3: 124
avocados 2: 61; 4: 225, 229;
    5: 251; 9: *520*
azaleas 10: 558
azobe 1: 3

bacteria 1: **28**, *28*; 2: 52;
    3: 140–141, 151, 163–164;
    4: 205, 233; 5: 240, 273;
    7: 415; 9: 508;
    10: 553–554, 561, 582
balsa 10: 575
bamboo 9: 518; 10: 558
bananas 4: 219, 225–226, *225*;
    5: 251; 8: 454
    plantains 4: 225
baobab flowers 5: *254*
bauhinias 9: 508
beeches 7: 406; 9: 516
    silky 10: 551
birch 7: 390
black booyong 10: 551
bladderworts 1: 28
blood vine 10: 551
blush tulip oak 10: 551
Brazil nut trees 3: 170
Brazil nuts 4: 196, 206, 230
breadfruit 4: 228; 5: 251, *251*
bromeliads 1: 8; 2: 59, **64**, *64*,
        69, 78–79, 89, 99–100;
    3: 120, 139, 155, 162;
    4: 183–184, *183*; 7: 391;
    8: 451, 478; 9: 507, 513;

10: 571, 576, 581, 599
    tank 4: *202*
buttress roots 3: 170, *170*;
    9: 507, 509, *509*; 10: 573,
    573

cacao 2: 55, *55*; 4: 219,
        228–229, *229*; 10: 585
cacti 10: 581
carnivorous plants 2: **88–89**,
        88–89; 7: 415; 8: 449,
        451
    bladderworts 2: 89
    bog violets 2: 89
    pitchers (SEE pitcher
        plants)
    sundews 2: 88–89, *89*
casaurina 7: 390
cassava, or manioc 4: 230;
    9: 510
ceiba (capok, kapok, or silk
        cotton) 3: 170–171; 6: 331;
    8: 453
cellulose 3: 140
chestnut 7: 390
chicle 9: 517
cinchona 4: 196; 7: 373
cinnamon tree 7: 390
climbers 3: **116–117**, 165;
        8: 449–451
    Marantia 8: *450*
    passionflowers 8: *449*, 452
    peperomias 8: 450
cocoa 8: 454 (SEE ALSO cacao)
coffee 4: 226–227; 8: 454
conifers 7: 412–413
crow's ash 10: 551
cycads 9: 508

Derris 9: 507, 510
Dinizia excelsa 3: 170
dipterocarps 1: 24; 3: 171, *171*;
    4: 187; 9: *519*; 10: 573–574,
    574

dormancy 3: 153; 9: 519;
    10: 574
Douglas fir 7: 412; 10: 557
dumbcanes, or diffenbachias
    10: 591
durian 5: 251; 9: 520–521

ebony 1: 4; 3: 124, 146; 8: 459;
    10: 575
emergents 3: 165, **170–171**;
    10: 572, *573*
epiphylls 8: 451, *451*; 9: 524,
    524; 10: 583
epiphytes 2: 64, 78, 99–100;
    3: 117, 120; 4: **183–184**,
    183–184, 189; 6: 328;
    7: 393; 8: 424–425,
    424–425, 444, 449, 476,
    478; 9: 507–508, 510;
    10: 551–552, 576, 581, 585,
    599
eucalyptus 1: 27; 4: 188, *188*;
    8: 455; 9: 496; 10: 571,
    571, 575

ferns 2: 100; 4: 183–184, 191,
        208–209; 5: 240; 7: 412;
        8: 451–453; 9: 508, 523;
        10: 553, 571, 581, 599
    adder's-tongue 4: 209
    bird's nest 3: 162; 4: 209;
        10: 551
    bracket 4: 209
    coral 4: *209*
    elephant 4: 208
    hare's foot 4: 209
    potato 4: 209
    ribbon 4: 209
    staghorn 4: *208*, 209
figs 3: 165, *165*; 4: *232*; 5: 251;
    10: 580
flame-of-the-forest 7: 390, *390*
flowering plants 4: 189–193,
    219–222

Boldface numbers before colons indicate volumes; boldface numbers following colons indicate whole articles; *italic* numbers are the page numbers of illustrations.

food web **4: 231–233**

foods **4: 225–230**

fruit **3:** 117; **5: 250–251**, 275–276; **9:** 521; **10:** 575, 585 (for species, see individual entries)

fungi **1:** 46–47, *47*; **2:** 52, 96; **3:** 140–141, *141*, 162–164 ; **4:** 233; **5:** 240–241, **252–253**, 285; **7:** 415; **8:** 451; **9:** 487, 507–508; **10:** 549, 553–554, *553*, 561, 572, 582

    candle snuff **5:** 253

    cookeina **5:** *252*, 253

    granadilla **4:** 229

    inky caps **5:** 253

    maiden's veil stinkhorn **5:** 253, *253*

    marasmius **5:** 253

    Phillipsia cup **5:** 241

    puff balls **5:** 253

fungus gardens **5:** 252–253

gedu nohor **1:** 3

gewa **7:** 362

giant Amazon water lily **4:** 217, 219, 221, *221*; **8:** 453, *453*

giant redwoods **10:** 557, *557*

giant stinging tree **6:** 324, *324* **10:** 583

gingers **4:** 219–221, *219*; **9:** 524 **10:** 591

ginkgo **10:** 558

goran **7:** 362

greenheart **10:** 575

guavas **4:** 225

heliconia, or crab claws **10:** 591, *591*

herbs **5:** 271 (SEE ALSO herbs and spices)

    lemongrass **5:** 271

    sweet basil **5:** 271

herbs and spices **5: 271–272**

hibiscus **4:** 221

hoop pines **10:** 551

hot-lips **4:** *220*; **9:** 524; **10:** 591

hurus **9:** 522

Indian rosewood **7:** 390

Intsia **9:** *509*

iroko (African teak) **1:** 4; **3:** 125, 146, 171; **4:** 195

Jack-in-the-pulpit **10:** 591

klinki pines **3:** 170–171

kola **4:** 230

laurels **10:** 558

leaves **6: 323–324**, *323*; **8:** 443–444, 449–453; **10:** 572, 583–584, 598

lianas **3:** 116–117, 121, 165; **4:** 196, 215, 221; **8:** 449, 451, *452*; **9:** 520–522; **10:** 571, 581, 590

    Alsomitra **9:** 522

    Macrozanonia macrocarpa **9:** 522

lichens **5:** 252; **6: 328–329**, *328–329*; **7:** 412; **8:** 449, 451, 478; **10:** 553, 571

    Parmelia **6:** 329

    Strigula **6:** 329

    Usnea **6:** 329

limes **4:** 228

liverworts (SEE mosses)

Macadamia **4:** 228

Mackay tulip oak **1:** 27

magnolia **7:** 390; **10:** 558

mahoganies **1:** 3; **4:** 180–181, 194; **6:** 331, 340; **7:** 390; **8:** 459; **9:** 488, 522; **10:** 575

mango **4:** 227–228; **9:** 520

mangosteen **4:** 227

mangroves **9:** 508–510, *510*, 522, *522*; **10:** 575

medicinal plants **3:** 148, 151, 157; **4:** 196–197; **7: 372–375**; **10:** 565, 575

    quinine **3:** 151

microorganisms **2:** 54–55;

6: 314; **10:** 553–554, 561

monkey puzzle trees **9:** 516

mora **9:** 522

mosses **2:** 100; **5:** 240; **7:** 390, **392–393**, *392–393*, 412; **8:** 449–452, 478; **10:** 571

    liverworts **7:** 393

    Spanish **4:** 184, *184*

mountain ebony **7:** 390

mycorrhizae **7:** 417, **8:** 425; **10:** 553, 572

nectar **2:** 56–57, 70, 71, 88; **3:** 116; **4:** 190, 205

nutmeg **7:** 390

okoume **1:** 4

oranges **4:** 227

orchids **2:** 78, 99–100; **3:** 162; **4:** 183–184, 189, 222, 227, 229; **5:** 285; **7:** 390; **8: 424–425**, *424–425*, 459–460; **9:** 507–508, 510, 519, 521, 536; **10:** 552, 571, 581

    Christmas star **8:** 424

    Dendrophylax **8:** 425

palms **1:** 24; **8: 428–429**, 477; **9:** 509, 520, *521*, 522 **10:** 590, *590*

    bottle **4:** 190

    climbing **3:** 116–117

    coco de mer **9:** 519

    coconut **8:** 428–429

    date **8:** 428

    nipa **7:** 362

    oil **1:** 4; **3:** 124; **4:** 226, *226*; **8:** 428–429, *428*, 454

    rattans (SEE rattans)

    sago **4:** 228; **5:** 289, *289*; **8:** 429, *429*

    talipot **8:** 428–429

papayas, or pawpaw, or papaw **4:** 229

parasites

    mistletoes **8:** 430–431, *431*

Boldface numbers before colons indicate volumes; **boldface** numbers following colons indicate whole articles; *italic* numbers are the page numbers of illustrations.

642

Parkia 4: 221

passionflowers 4: 220; 8: *449, 450, 452*

passionfruit 4: 229, *232*

peanuts 4: 230

peperomias 9: 509

peppers 4: 229

photosynthesis 2: 64, 80–81; 3: 115; 6: 323, 328–329; 8: 425, 431, **443–444**, *443,* 449–450; 9: 509–510, 519–520, 523–524; 10: 553, 572, 574

pineapples 4: 229; 5: 251;

pines 7: 390, 406
    matai, or black pine 7: 406
    rimu, or red pine 7: 406

pitcher plants 1: 24, 28; 2: 88–89, *88*
    phial pitcher 2: 89
    raja pitcher 2: 88
    yellow trumpet 2: 89

plantations 4: 176, 178; 6: 301
    banana 2: 99–100, *101;* 8: *454*
    cacao 4: 229
    oil palm 4: 178, 181, 226
    rubber 4: 178, 196, *196*
    tree 3: 128, 147, 171; 8: *455*

plants, general 8: 443–444, **449–453**; 9: 523–524, 536 (for species, see individual entries)

plum trees 7: 390

pollination 2: 56–57, 64, 78; 3: 128, 162–163; 4: 190, 196, 219–222; 6: 305, 315; 8: 424–425, 431, **460–462**, *460–462,* 479; 10: 572

quinine 4: 196

rafflesias 1: 24; 4: 220; 8: 431, 451, 473, *473*; 9: 520

rambutans 4: 227; 5: *250*; 9: 520

rata 7: 406; 8: 476

rattans 1: 24; 3: 117; 8: 428, **479–480**, *479–480*

red cedars 10: 557

rice 4: 228

roots 7: 362–363; 9: **507–510**; 10: 549, 553, 571, 573, 581, 597–598

rose mahogany 10: 551

rose satinash 10: 551

rosy periwinkle 2: 54–55; 4: 196; 7: 375, *375*

rubber 1: 4; 3: 147; 8: 454; 9: 496–497, **511–512**, *511–512*

saffron heart 10: 551

sandalwood 7: 390; 8: 459

sapele (African mahogany) 1: 3–4; 3: 124, 146, 171; 10: 575

sapodilla 4: 225–226

seed dispersal 5: 250–251

seeds 2: 56–58, 61; 9: 488, **519–522**, 524, 536; 10: 557, 573–574, 584–585

shade toleration 3: 162; 6: 324; 9: **523–524**

Shorea 10: 572

Sitka spruce 3: 153; 7: 412; 10: 557

Sonneratia 7: 362

spices 4: 227–228; 5: **271–272**, 10: 575
    cinnamon 4: 227; 5: 272
    cloves 4: 227; 5: 271, 272
    ginger 4: 227; 5: 272
    mace 4: 227
    nutmeg 4: 227; 5: 272
    pepper 4: 227; 5: 271–272
    vanilla 4: 229; 5: 272, *272*; 8: 424

strangler figs 3: 117; 8: 451; 9: 507, 509; 10: 585, *585*

succession 5: 243

sugarcane 1: 45; 4: 228

sundri 7: 362

sweet potatoes 4: 230

Swiss-cheese plants 3: 117; 9: 509, 520; 10: 591

teak 3: 146–147, 171; 4: 194; 6: 331, 340, 342; 7: 389; 8: *455, 455*; 9: *488, 518*; 10: 575

thismia 4: 220

tree ferns 10: 575

tree nurseries 9: *486, 487–489, 488–489*

trees 7: 389; 9: 486–489, 501, 507–510, 516–522; 10: 549, 551, 553, 557, 559, **570–575**, 590
    hardwoods 3: 124–125, 128, 146, 148–149
    softwoods 3: 147
    (for species, see individual entries)

truffles 10: 549

tualangs 3: 171; 10: 572

underwater 8: 452

upas trees 5: 289

utile 1: 3

vanilla (SEE spices)

violets, African 1: 3; 3: 124; 8: 444

western hemlock 7: 412; 10: 557

western red cedar 7: 412

white beefwood 10: 551

yams 4: 228

Boldface numbers before colons indicate volumes; **boldface** numbers following colons indicate whole articles; *italic* numbers are the page numbers of illustrations.

Reptiles and Amphibians Index

alligators **6**: 336, 339
amphibians **1**: 7, **8–9**; **9**: 516, 537; **10**: 593 (for species, see individual entries)
anoles **3**: 122; **6**: *334*, 335; **9**: 492

Boyd's forest dragon **9**: *490*

caecilians **1**: 8, *8*; **10**: 593
caimans (SEE crocodilians)
chameleons **1**: 4, 45; **2**: 75, 85, **102**, *102*; **4**: 204, 207, *207*; **6**: 309, 333–334; **9**: 491
    panther **1**: *42*
    Parson's **1**: *42*
cobras **3**: **118–119**, *118–119*
communication **3**: **121–123**, *122*
courtship **3**: **132–133**
crocodilians **3**: **134–137**; **4**: 206, 232; **7**: 405, 408; **9**: 490–491, 502; **10**: 594
    caimans **2**: 84–85; **3**: 134–137
        black **3**: 137
        dwarf, or smooth-fronted **3**: *135*, 137
        spectacled **2**: 85; **3**: *134*, 136
    crocodiles **2**: 84–85, *85*
        dwarf crocodiles **9**: *491*
        Johnston's, or freshwater **3**: *135*, 136
        mugger, or marsh **3**: *135*, *137*
        New Guinea **3**: 135, *135*
        saltwater, or estuarine **3**: *135*, *135*
        West African dwarf **3**: 135

frogs **2**: 64, 74, 89; **3**: 121, 132–133, 163; **7**: 408; **10**: 571, 592, 593–594, 598–599 (SEE ALSO frogs and toads)
    American nest-building **1**: 9
    common mantella **1**: 43
    flying **5**: 249; **6**: 338
    foam nest **7**: 404
    gastric brooding **1**: 27
    glass **1**: 9; **2**: 74; **10**: 576–577, *577*
    golden **1**: *43*
    goliath **1**: 5; **5**: 248, *248*
    horned
        Malaysian horned **2**: *74*; **5**: 248–249
    leaf **10**: 576–577
    marsupial **10**: 577
    poison dart **1**: 9; **5**: 246–248, *247*; **8**: 457; **10**: 576–577, *576*
    psyllophryne didactyla **5**: 247
    pygmy marsupial **1**: 9
    red-eyed leaf **1**: 9; **3**: *132*; **5**: *246*, *247*; **6**: *336*; **7**: 399
    reed **10**: 577
    Sarayacu **1**: 7, *7*
    tree **1**: 4, 8, 9; **2**: 74, 79; **5**: 246, 249; **6**: *336*; **10**: 576–577, 593
    whistling **5**: 248
frogs and toads **1**: 8–9; **5**: **246–249**; **6**: 308, 336–337, 339; **9**: 502
    camouflage **5**: 249
    poisonous **5**: 246–247, 249
    reproduction **5**: 247–249

geckos **5**: **255–256**; **6**: **332–336**
    dwarf **5**: 255

flying **5**: 255, *255*
    green day **5**: 256, *256*
    leaf-tailed **5**: 256
        Madagascan leaf-tailed **9**: *490*, 491
    naked-fingered **5**: 256
    tokay **5**: 256; **6**: *332*, 333
    turnip-tailed **5**: 256

iguanas **2**: 100; **3**: 165; **5**: 294–295; **6**: 332, 334–335
    basilisks **5**: 295, *295*; **6**: 335–336
    green, or common **4**: *232*; **5**: 294–295, *294*; **6**: 334

Jacobson's organs **6**: 333

lizards **3**: *122*, 123, 141; **4**: 206; **6**: 308–309, **332–335**, 336; **9**: 490–492, *490*, 518; **10**: 571, 594
    anoles (SEE anoles)
    chisel-teeth **9**: 492
    flying **1**: 24; **6**: 338, *338*
    geckos (SEE geckos)
    iguanas (SEE iguanas)
    Komodo dragons **6**: 333, *333*
    monitors **6**: 332, 334–335
    nose-horned **9**: 491
    skinks (SEE skinks)
    worm **6**: 335, *335*

newts **10**: 593

pythons (SEE snakes)

reptiles, general **3**: 118–119, 134–137; **9**: **490–493**; **10**: 594 (for species, see individual entries)

Boldface numbers before colons indicate volumes; **boldface** numbers following colons indicate whole articles; *italic* numbers are the page numbers of illustrations.

salamanders **1**: 8; **2**: 79; **6**: 339; **9**: **513**, 516; **10**: 571, 593, 598–599, *599*

skinks **6**: 335
  blue-tongued **6**: 335
  Brazilian **6**: 334
  marine **6**: 333
  Murray's forest **1**: 27
  orange-sided **1**: 27

snakes **4**: 206; **6**: 336, 338; **7**: 407–408; **9**: 490–493, **530–533**; **10**: 571, 594
  anaconda **2**: 84, *84*, **3**: 130; **9**: 530
  blind **9**: 531
  boa **3**: 130–131; **4**: *232*; **7**: 407–408; **9**: 531
    rainbow **3**: *130*, 131
  bushmasters **9**: 530, 532
  camouflage **2**: 75; **3**: 131
  cobras **9**: 531–532; **3**: **118–119**, *118–119*;
    king cobras **1**: 25; **9**: 490, 533
  constrictors **3**: **130–131**
  coral **9**: 492, *531*, 532
  fer-de-lance **9**: *492*, 493, 531
  flowerpot **9**: 530
  flying **9**: 533
  kraits **3**: 119
  mussuranas **9**: 531
  nesting **3**: 119
  parrot **9**: *530*
  pipe **9**: 532
  pythons **2**: 84; **3**: 119, 130–131; **4**: *232*; **9**: 491, 530–533, *533*
    green tree **3**: 131, *131*
    Indian **3**: 130; **9**: 531, 533
    reticulated **1**: *24*, 25; **9**: 531
    ringed **3**: 131
  rat **3**: 119
  tree **9**: 532–533
  venom **3**: 118–119

vine **9**: 530, 532, *532*
vipers **9**: 531, 533
  eyelash **5**: 287; **9**: *491*
  gaboon **1**: 5, *5*; **3**: 125; **9**: 493
  jumping **9**: 530
  lichen **9**: 492
toads, general (SEE frogs and toads)
  African clawed **1**: 9
  fire-bellied **1**: 9
  giant, or cane **4**: 233; **5**: 246, 249, *249*
  golden **2**: 99, *99*
  horned **1**: 9
  Surinam, or pipa **1**: 9; **5**: 248
tortoises (SEE turtles and terrapins)
tree frogs (SEE frogs)
turtles and terrapins **3**: 141; **4**: 181; **9**: 490–491, 493, 502; **10**: **586–589**, 594
  African hingeback **10**: 587
  arau river **10**: 588
  Chinese box **10**: *589*
  Cuora box **10**: 587
  hinge-backed tortoises **9**: *491*
  matamata **10**: 587
  mud **10**: 587–588
    scorpion mud **10**: *588*
  musk **10**: 589
  red-eared terrapins **10**: *586*, 589
  river **4**: 181
  sidenecked, or snake-necked **10**: 587
  snapping **10**: 588
  softshells **10**: 588
  spiny hill tortoises **9**: 493, *493*
  yellow-footed tortoises **4**: 181

vipers (SEE snakes)

Boldface numbers before colons indicate volumes; **boldface** numbers following colons indicate whole articles; *italic* numbers are the page numbers of illustrations.

Research and Conservation Index

African Timber Organization 1: 5
agriculturalists 2: 83
anthropologists 2: 82

biomass 2: 52–53
biotechnology 2: 54–55, 54
botanists 2: 82–83
bush meat 2: 105; 3: 125;
    4: 181

canopy, researching the
    2: 76–77
carbon dioxide 2: 80–81;
    3: 115, 148
careers 2: 82–83
cattle ranching 2: 94–95, 94,
    100, 108–109; 3: 147;
    4: 180, 187, 195; 6: 343;
    7: 380; 9: 497, 538
clear-cutting 2: 108–109, 108;
    5: 242; 6: 340, 341–342,
    344; 7: 411; 8: 472
climate, world 2: 80–81; 3: 115;
    9: 487, 515
conservation 1: 5; 2: 99, 101;
    3: 126–129, 141; 4: 197;
    5: 242, 283; 9: 487–488
Convention on International
    Trade in Endangered
    Species of Wild Fauna and
    Flora (CITES) 9: 529

dams (SEE ALSO
    hydroelectricity)
    3: 147–148, 151–152;
    5: 290–291
    Turucui dam 5: 291
deforestation 2: 52–53, 55,
    80–81, 94–95, 108–109;
    3: 125, 146–149, 171;
    4: 176–178, 180–182, 185,
    187, 194–195, 203;
    5: 238–239, 260–263, 285;
    6: 301, 340–345, 348–349;

7: 363, 363, 380;
    9: 486–489, 496, 536, 538;
    10: 559, 581, 583

ecotourism (SEE tourism)
endangered species 1: 5, 7, 45;
    2: 63, 86–87, 92;
    3: 126–129, 135–136, 145,
    161; 4: 176–182;
    6: 348–349; 9: 498, 529,
    536; 10: 563
erosion 4: 185–188, 185–186;
    5: 242; 6: 341, 348; 7: 380;
    10: 599, 601
ethnobotanists 3: 157
exploitation 4: 194–197
exploration and research
    4: 198–201
extinction 1: 45; 2: 63, 99;
    3: 146–148; 4: 176–178,
    181, 202–203; 8: 458;
    9: 498, 536; 10: 563

farming 1: 4–5, 7; 2: 53, 55, 83,
    94–95, 100, 105; 3: 125,
    128–129, 147–148;
    5: 244–245, 262, 282–283,
    292–293; 6: 301, 322;
    9: 486–487, 494–495, 494,
    525–526, 526; 10: 575
Fauna and Flora Preservation
    Society 4: 201
forest fires 2: 95, 95;
    5: 238–239, 238–239, 243
forestry 2: 83, 5: 242–245
    agroforestry 5: 244–245,
    244
    artificial regeneration
    5: 244
    natural regeneration
    5: 243–244
    seed orchards 5: 245
    selective felling 5: 242–243
Friends of the Earth 4: 201

game wardens 2: 83
genetic engineering 2: 54–55
global warming 2: 81; 3: 115,
    148; 5: 260–263, 282, 291;
    8: 464, 477; 9: 487
Grand Carajas Program 7: 381
greenhouse effect 5: 260–261

human interference 5: 282–283
hunting 9: 495
hydroelectricity 6: 320;
    7: 380–381; 9: 497, 502,
    538; 10: 601
hydrologists 2: 82

International Tropical Timber
    Organization (ITTO) 1: 5;
    6: 341

keystone species 3: 165

logging 1: 3–5; 2: 100, 105,
    108–109, 109; 3: 125, 129,
    147. 149, 157; 4: 178, 181,
    194–195, 201; 5: 282;
    6: 301, 340–345;
    7: 379–380; 8: 455, 463;
    9: 496, 538; 10: 559, 565,
    575, 599

Malayan Nature Society 4: 201
meteorologists 2: 82
mining 1: 7; 3: 129, 148,
    151–152; 4: 195; 5: 282;
    6: 301; 7: 378–381,
    378–381; 8: 463, 465;
    9: 487, 495, 496–497, 538;
    10: 605
mud slides 4: 188

naturalists 3: 127–128

Nigerian Conservation
    Foundation 4: 201

Boldface numbers before colons indicate volumes; boldface numbers following colons indicate whole articles; italic numbers are the page numbers of illustrations.

oil exploration **4**: 181; **5**: 283; **7**: **416–417**; **8**: 463–464; **9**: 496
Omere Wiki Foundation **2**: 101

park rangers **2**: 82–83; **4**: 181
plantations **8**: *428*, 429, **454–455**, *454–455*; **9**: 486, 496–497, 511–512; **10**: 559, 575
poaching **2**: 63, 109; **3**: 128; **4**: 178–179; **5**: 282; **7**: 418; **8**: **456–459**, *456–459*
podologists **2**: 82
pollution **3**: 152; **5**: 238, 283, *283*; **7**: 379, 417; **8**: **463–465**, *463–465*; **9**: 487, 496; **10**: 599, 605

reforestation **2**: 101; **4**: 188, *188*; **5**: 263; **9**: **486–489**
research, general **4**: **198–200**
road building **3**: 129, 148; **4**: 181, 186–187, 195; **6**: 341, *342*, 343; **9**: 496

scientific research **2**: 76–77, 82–83
slash and burn **1**: 4, 21; **3**: 147; **4**: 187, 195; **5**: 262, 292; **6**: 321, 348; **7**: 368, 380; **8**: 464; **9**: **525–526**, *525–526*; **10**: 604

tourism **2**: 82–83, 99, 101 **3**: 128–129, 137; **4**: 182; **5**: 245, 266, 280, *282*; **7**: 396–400; **8**: 458, *463*; **9**: 537; **10**: **568–569**
tree nurseries **9**: *486*, 487–489, *488–489*
Tropical Forest Research Centre **4**: 201
Tropical Forestry Action Plan **4**: 201

United Nations Environment Programme **3**: 127

Wet Tropics World Heritage Area **1**: 27
Wildlife Conservation International **4**: 201
World Conservation Monitoring Centre **3**: 127; **4**: 176
World Conservation Union (IUCN) **3**: 127; **4**: 201
World Forestry Congress **4**: 201
World Wide Fund for Nature (WWF) **3**: 127, 129; **4**: 201

zoologists **2**: 82–83

Boldface numbers before colons indicate volumes; **boldface** numbers following colons indicate whole articles; *italic* numbers are the page numbers of illustrations.

Scientific Names Index

Mammals

African elephant (*Loxodonta africana*) **3**: 169; **6**: 331, 355

Amazonian manatee (*Trichechus inunguis*) **4**: 181; **6**: *357*

Asiatic black bear (*Ursus thibetanus*) **7**: 397

Asian elephants (*Elephas maximus*) **1**: 25; **3**: 169; **5**: 274

Axis deer (*Axis axis*) **3**: *143, 144*

Aye-aye (*Daubentonia madagascariensis*) **1**: 4; **4**: *206*; **6**: 348, 349, 354; **7**: 408

Bali tiger (*Panthera tigris balica*) **10**: 563

Bearded pig (*Sus barbartus*) **7**: *376*; **8**: 445

Black-and-white colobus (*Colobus guereza*) **7**: 398

Black bear (*Ursus americanus*) **1**: 33, **10**: *558*

Black lemur (*Eulemur macaco*) **6**: 326, 327

Blue-eyed lemur (*Eulemur macaco flavifrons*) **8**: 468

Bongo antelope (*Tragelaphus euryceros*) **1**: *14*

Bonnet macaque (*Macaca radiata*) **7**: 390

Bonobo chimpanzee (*Pan paniscus*) **1**:17; **2**: *104*

Boto/pink river dolphin (*Inia geoffrensis*) **3**: 152, *152*

Buffy-headed marmoset (*Callithrix flaviceps*) **4**: 180

Bush dog (*Speothos venaticus*) **2**: 86, *86*

Capuchin monkey (*Cebus capuccinus*) **4**: 232

Capybara (*Hydrochaeris hydrochaeris*) **4**: 232; **5**: *275*; **6**: 339, 353, *355*; **9**: *503, 504, 505*, 536

Caspian tiger (*Panthera tigris virgata*) **10**: 563

Cheetah (*Acinonyx jubatus*) **2**: 86

Chimpanzee (*Pan troglodytes*) **1**: 2, 4, 16–17, *17*; **2**: 103–105, *103*; **3**: 125, 129, 165; **4**: 193, 231; **6**: 337; **7**: 399, 405

Chinese tiger (*Panthera tigris amoyensis*) **10**: 563

Clouded leopard (*Neofelis nebulosa*) **2**:*93*; **8**: 457

Crested porcupine (*Hystrix cristata*) **9**: 506

DeBrazza's monkey (*Cercopithecus neglectus*) **7**: 385

Diademed sifaka (*Propithecus diadema*) **1**: 42

Douglas squirrel (*Tamiasciurus douglasii*) **10**: 548

Douroucouli/night monkey (*Aotus trivirgatus*) **7**: 388, 407, 408

Dugong (*Dugong dugon*) **6**: 357; **9**: 502

Eastern lowland gorilla (*Gorilla graueri*) **3**: 125; **5**: 264, 265

Echidna/spiny anteater (*Tachyglossus aculeatus*) **6**: 353

Emperor tamarin (*Saguinus imperator*) **7**: 367, *367*

Fishing bat (*Noctilio leporinus*) **1**: *30*

Fishing cat (*Felis viverrina*) **2**: 90, 93

Fringe-lipped bat (*Trachops cirrhosus*) **1**: 31

Fruit bat (*Pteropus giganteus*) **1**: 4

Gaur (*Bos gaurus*) **4**: 176

Giant anteater (*Myrmecophaga tridactyla*) **1**: 13

Giant forest hog (*Hylochoerus meinertzhageni*) **8**: 446, *446*

Giant otter (*Pteronura brasiliensis*) **5**: 257, *257*

Golden bamboo lemur (*Hapalemur aureus*) **4**: 176

Golden lion tamarin (*Leontopithecus rosalia*) **4**:180; **7**: 367

Golden potto/angwantibo (*Artocebus calabarensis*) **6**: 346

Gray fox (*Urocyon cinereoargenteus*) **2**: 86

Grizzly bear (*Ursus arctos*) **1**: 33

Hairy-legged vampire bat (*Diphylla ecaudata*) **1**: 30

Honduran white bat (*Ectophylla alba*) **1**: 31

Howler monkey (*Alouatta palliata*) **2**: 79; **3**: 123, *123*; **7**: 386–387

Indian Tiger (*Panthera tigris tigris*) **10**: 562, 563

Boldface numbers before colons indicate volumes; numbers following colons indicate pages; *italic* numbers are the page numbers of illustrations.

Indri (*Indri indri*) **1**: 4, 42; **3**: 147; **6**: 327, 337

Iriomote Cat (*Prionailurus bengalensis*) **2**: 92

Jaguar (*Panthera onca*) **2**: 85, 86, 90, *91*, 92, 100; **4**: 232–233; **6**: *316*, 336, 354

Jaguarundi (*Felis yaguarondi*) **2**: 86, 92, 93

Javan rhinoceros (*Rhinoceros sondaicus*) **4**: 178; **6**: 302; **9**: 498

Javan tiger (*Panthera tigris sondaica*) **10**: 563

Kitti's hog-nosed bat (*Craseonycteris thonglongyai*) **1**: 30; **6**: 352

Kloss's gibbon (*Hylobates klossii*) **5**: 259

Lesser galago (*Galago senegalensis*) **5**: *254*

Lesser mouse deer (*Tragulus javanicus*) **6**: 302

Lion-tailed macaque (*Macaca silenus*) **1**: 25

Long-tailed macaque (*Macaca fuscicularis*) **6**: 301

Malayan tapir (*Tapirus indicus*) **10**: *555*

Mandrill (*Mandrillus sphinx*) **7**: 387

Margay (*Felis wiedi*) **2**: 93, 100

Mountain gorilla (*Gorilla Berengei*) **1**: 16, 45; **4**: 182; **5**: 264; **7**: *405*

Muriqui (*Brachyteles arachnoides*) **4**: 180–181; **9**: 536

Nine-banded armadillo (*Dasypus novemcinctus*) **1**: 19, *19*

Northern flying squirrel (*Glaucomys sabrinus*) **7**: 412, *412*

Northern tamandua (*Tamandua mexicana*) **1**: 13

Numbat (*Myrmecobius Fasciatus*) **4**: 207

Ocelot (*Felis pardalis*) **2**: 93, 100

Okapi (*Giraffa camelopardalis*) **1**: 28, 45; **3**: 125; **4**: 205; **6**: 355; **7**: *418*

Olympic marmot (*Marmota olympus*) **10**: 549

Orangutan (*Pongo pygmaeus*) **1**: 16–18; **3**: 163; **4**: *177*, 178; **6**: 302–303; **7**: 405, *419*

Palm civet (*Chrotogale owstoni*) **2**: *107*

Pig-tailed macaque (*Macaca nemistring*) **1**: 25, **7**: 385

Proboscis monkey (*Nasalis larvatus*) **6**: *301*, 302; **7**: 386, *386*

Pygmy hippopotamus (*Choeropsis liberiensis*) **1**: 4

Pygmy marmoset (*Callithrix pygmaea*) **7**: 366

Red brocket deer (*Mazama americana*) **3**: 144–145, *144*

Red colobus monkey (*Procolobus badius*) **1**: 4; **5**: 273; **7**: 398

Red-bellied lemur (*Eulemur rubriventer*) **1**: *43*

Red-fronted lemur (*Eulemur fulvus*) **1**: *43*

Red panda (*Ailurus fulgens*) **8**: 481, *481*

Red river hog (*Potamochoerus porcus*) **8**: 458

Red-ruffed lemur (*Varecia variegata*) **6**: 349

Rhesus monkey (*Macaca mulatta*) **7**: 388

Ring-tailed mongoose (*Galidia elegans*) **7**: 384

Roosevelt elk (*Cervus elaphus roosevelti*) **7**: *413*

Royal antelope (*Neotragus pygmaeus*) **1**: 15

Rufous mouse lemur (*Microcebus rufus*) **8**: 468–469

Rusa deer (*Cervus timorensis*) **6**: 302

Saddle-back tamarin (*Saguinus fuscicollis*) **7**: 367

Sambar (*Cervus unicolour*) **1**: 25; **3**: 142, 145; **7**: 390; **9**: *517*

Scaly-tailed squirrel (*Zenkerella insignis*) **9**: 505; **10**: 549

Short-tailed fruit bat (*Carollia perspicillata*) **1**: 32

Siamang gibbon (*Hylobates syndactylus*) **1**: 18; **5**: 258, *258*

Siberian tiger (*Panthera tigris altaica*) **10**: 563

Silky anteater (*Cyclopes didactylus*) **1**: 13; **4**: 232; **6**: 309, *309*

Slender loris (*Loris tardigradus*) **6**: *346*

Sloth bear (*Melursus ursinus*) **1**: 33, *33*

Slow loris (*Nycticebus coucang*) **6**: 346; **7**: 408

Spider monkey (*Ateles geoffroyi*) **2**: 79; **7**: 385

Boldface numbers before colons indicate volumes; numbers following colons indicate pages; *italic* numbers are the page numbers of illustrations.

Spot-nosed monkey (*Cercopithecus nictitans*) 8: 459

Squirrel monkey (*Saimiri sciureus*) 7: 387; 8: 469

Stripe-necked mongoose (*Hyaenidae Proteles cristatus*) 7: 384

Sumatran rhinoceros (*Dicerorhinus sumatrensis*) 4: *178*; 6: *302*; 9: *498*

Sumatran tiger (*Panthera tigris sumatrae*) 10: *563*

Sun bear (*Helarctos malayanus*) 1: 33; 2: 85, 87

Suni antelope (*Neotragus moschatus*) 3: 160

Susus dolphin (*Platanista minor*) 3: 152

Three-banded armadillo (*Tolypeutes tricinctus*) 1: 19

Titi monkey (*Callicebus moloch*) 7: 387

Toque macaque (*Macaca Sinica*) 1: 25

Tree porcupine (*Erethizon dorsatum*) 9: *506*

Tree shrew (*Tupaia glis*) 6: *356*

Tube-nosed bat (*Nyctimene rabori*) 1: *32*

Vampire bat (*Desmodus rotundus*) 1: 30; 2: 100; 4: 205

Visayan spotted deer (*Cervus alfredi*) 3: 145

Water chevrotain (*Hyemoschus aquaticus*) 1: 5

West African manatee (*Trichechus senegalensis*) 6: 357

Western lowland gorilla (*Gorilla gorilla*) 1: *16*; 5: *264*; 7: *399*

West Indian manatee (*Trichechus manatus*) 6: 357

White-nosed coati (*Nasua narica*) 6: *355*

White tent-building bat (*Uroderma bilobatum*) 2: 78

White-winged vampire bat (*Diaemus youngi*) 1: 30

Marsupials

Black tree kangaroo (*Dendrolagus ursinus*) 10: 579

Doria tree kangaroo (*Dendrolagus dorianus*) 10: 579

Honey possum (*Tarsipes rostratus*) 3: 163; 4: 205; 5: 273, 276; 6: 353

Muskrat kangaroo (*Hypsiprymnodon moschatus*) 1: 27

Red-necked pademelon (*Thylogale thetis*) 10: 551

Plants, Algae, and Microorganisms

African baobab flower (*Adansonia digitata*) 5: 254

Amazon water lily (*Victoria amazonica*) 4: **217**, 219, 221; 8: 453

Australian hare's-foot fern (*Davallia pyxidata*) 4: 209

Bird-of-paradise flower (*Strelitzia reginae*) 1: *3*, 4; 8: 462

Black booyong (*Argyrodendron actinophyllum*) 10: 551

Black tree fern (*Cyathea medullaris*) 8: 474

Blush tulip oak (*Argyrodendron actinophyllum*) 10: 551

Bracket fern (*Pteridium esculentum*) 4: 209

Catestum (*Catasetum saccatum*) 4: 222

Cookeina fungus (*Cookeina colensoi*) 5: 252

Coral fern (*Gleichenia microphylla*) 4: 209

Crow's ash (*Flindersia australis*) 10: 551

Double coconut (*Lodoicea maldivica*) 8: 428

Elephant ear fern (*Elaphoglossum crinitum*) 4: 208

Flame-of-the-forest tree (*Delonix regia*) 7: 390

Hare's foot fern (*Davallia mariesii*) 4: 209

Hot-lips (*Chelone lyonii*) 4: 220; 9: 524; 10: 591

Jack-in-the-pulpit (*Arisaema triphyllum*) 10: 591

Mackay tulip oak (*Argyrodendron actinophyllum*) 1: 27

Maiden's veil stinkhorn (*Dictyophora duplicata*) 5: 253

Matai/black pine (*Prumnopitys taxifolia*) 7: 406; 8: 476

Boldface numbers before colons indicate volumes; numbers following colons indicate pages; *italic* numbers are the page numbers of illustrations.

Monkey puzzle tree (*Araucaria araucana*) **9**: 516

Passionflower (*Passiflora incarnata*) **4**: 220; **8**: *449, 450, 452*

Potato fern (*Marratia salicina*) **4**: 209

Rambutan (*Nephelium lappaceum*) **4**: 227; **5**: 250; **9**: 520

Red cedar (*Toona australis*) **10**: 557

Rose satinash (*Eugenia francisii*) **10**: 551

Sago palm (*Cycas revoluta*) **4**: 228; **5**: 289; **8**: 429

Sapodilla tree (*Manilkara achras*) **4**: 225–226

Silky beech (*Citronella smythii*) **10**: 551

Sitka spruce (*Picea sitchensis*) **3**:153; **7**: 412; **10**: 557

Staghorn fern (*Platycerium suberbum*) **4**: 208, 209

Strangler fig (*Ficus aurea*) **3**: 117; **8**: 451; **9**: 507, 509; **10**: 585

Streptomyces **1**: 28

Talipot palm (*Corypha umbraculifera*) **8**: 428–429

Teak (*Tectona grandis*) **3**: 146–147, 171; **4**: 194; **6**: 331, 340, 342; **7**: 389; **8**: 455; **9**: 488, 518; **10**: 575

Titan arum (*Amorphophallus titanum*) **4**: 222

Upas tree (*Antiaris toxicaria*) **5**: 289

Western hemlock (*Tsuga heterophylla*) **7**:412; **10**: 557

Birds

African gray parrot (*Psittacus erithacus*) **3**: 125; **8**: 432

Anhingas/snakebirds (*Anhinga anhinga*) **6**: 339

Argus pheasant (*Argusianus argus*) **3**: 122

Asian fairy bluebird (*Irena puella*) **7**: 397

Bare-necked umbrella bird (*Cephalopterus glabricollis*) **2**: 99

Bee hummingbird (*Mellisuga helenae*) **5**: 286

Black-headed caique (*Pionites melanocephala*) **2**: 58

Bluebottle swallowtail (*Graphium sarpedon*) **2**: 71

Cassowary (*Casuarius casuarius*) **1**: 27, **2**: 57; **3**: 122; **10**: 594

Cock-of-the-rock (*Rupicola peruviana*) **3**: 132; **4**: 232

Crested honeycreeper (*Palmeria dolei*) **10**: 559

Crowned eagle (*Tephanoaetus coronatus*) **3**: 158–159, 165; **7**: 403

Crowned wood partridge (*Rollulus roulroul*) **8**: 445

Eungella honeyeater (*Lichenostomus hindwoodi*) **1**: 27

Giant hummingbird (*Patagona gigas*) **5**: 286

Great-billed parrot (*Tanygnathus megalorynchos*) **8**: 434

Great horned owl (*Bubo virginianus*) **8**: 426

Groove-billed toucanet (*Aulacorhynchus sulcatus*) **10**: 567

Harpy eagle (*Harpia harpyja*) **2**: 60, 79; **3**: 158–161, *161*; **4**: 232

Javan kingfisher (*Halcyon smyrnensis*) **6**: 303

Keel-billed toucan (*Ramphastos sulfuratus*) **10**: 566

King vulture (*Sarcoramphus papa*) **10**: 596

Maleo (*Macrocephalon maleo*) **2**: 60; **4**: 179

Military macaw (*Ara militaris*) **10**: 593

Milky eagle owl/Verreaux's eagle owl (*Bubo lacteus*) **2**: 59

Moluccan cockatoo (*Cacatua moluccensis*) **8**: 433

Orange-winged Amazon parrot (*Amazona amazonica*) **8**: 433

Papuan hawk owl (*Uroglaux dimorpha*) **8**: 427

Philippine/monkey-eating eagle (*Pithecophaga jefferyi*) **2**: 60; **3**: 158–161, *160*; **4**: 177; **5**: 282

Raggiana bird of paradise (*Paradisaea raggiana*) **2**: *63*

Boldface numbers before colons indicate volumes; numbers following colons indicate pages; *italic* numbers are the page numbers of illustrations.

Scientific Names Index

Rainbow lorikeet (*Trichoglossus haematodus*) **8**: *434*

Rainbow pitta (*Pitta iris*) **7**: *405*

Red-capped manakin (*Pipra mentalis*) **10**: *594*

Resplendent quetzal (*Pharomacrus mocino*) **2**: *61, 99*; **5**: *251, 274*; **7**: *400*; **8**: *478*; **10**: *571*

Ruby-topaz hummingbird (*Apodifomes nectivores*) **5**: *287*

Salmon-crested cockatoo (*Cacatua moluccensis*) **8**: *432*

Scarlet macaw (*Ara macao*) **4**: *232*

Scarlet minivet (*Pericrocotus flammeus*) **7**: *397*

Slender-billed cockatoo (*Cacatua pastinator*) **8**: *433*

Sooty owl (*Tyto tenebricosa*) **7**: *409*; **8**: *426*

Spectacled owl (*Pulsatrix perspicillata*) **8**: *427*

Spotted owl (*Strix occidentalis*) **2**: *61*; **4**: *182*; **10**: *558*

Three-wattled bellbird (*Procnias tricarunculata*) **2**: *99*

Toco toucan (*Ramphastos toco*) **10**: *552*

Tropical screech owl (*Otus choliba*) **8**: *426*

Yellow-green vireo (*Vireo flavoviridis*) **7**: *376*

Invertebrates

Aeshnid dragonfly (*Anax junius*) **3**: *154*

Army ants (*Eciton hamatum*) **1**: *10–11, 10*; **2**: *84*; **4**: *207, 231*; **5**: *241*

Australian chafer beetle (*Costelytra zealandica*) **1**: *39*

Botfly/warble fly (*Dermatobia hominis*) **4**:*223–224*

Click beetle (*Anostirus castaneus*) **1**: *37, 47*

Coconut crab (*Birgus latro*) **3**: *138*; **5**: *273*

Dung beetle (*Onthophagus australis*) **3**: *141*; **5**: *241*; **6**: *307, 314*

Emperor moth (*Saturnia pavonia*) **6**: *304*

Fiddle/violin beetle (*Carabidae mormolyce*) **1**: *39*

Goliath beetle (*Scarabaeidae goliathus*) **1**: *40*

Goliath tarantula (*Theraposa leblondi*) **6**: *310*; **8**: *438*; **9**: *539, 541, 543*

Harlequin beetle (*Acrocinus longimanus*) **4**: *232*; **6**: *307*

Heliconiid butterfly (*Dryas iulia*) **1**: *69*; **4**: *232*; **6**: *307*; **8**: *452*

Hercules beetle (*Dynastes hercules*) **1**: *40*

Isabella tiger butterfly (*Eueides isabella*) **6**: *315*

Kite spider (*Gasteracanthus sanguinolenta*) **9**: *539*

Leaf-cutter ant (*Atta cephelotes*) **1**: *11*; **3**: *162*; **5**: *253*; **10**: *553, 554*

Madagascan hissing cockroach (*Gromphadorhina portentosa*) **3**: *120*

Morpho butterfly (*Morpho mamnon*) **2**: *72*; **6**: *304*

Paper wasp (*Polistes fuscatus*) **1**: *34*; **7**: *403*

Potter wasp (*Symmorphus bifasciatus*) **7**: *403*

Queen Alexandra's bird wing (*Ornitoptera alexandrae*) **2**: *70*; **6**: *310*

Red land crab (*Gecardoidea natalis*) **3**: *139*

Robber fly (*Diptera asilidae*) **4**: *224*; **6**: *306, 307*

Robber crab (*Birgus latro*) **6**: *313*

Stag beetle (*Lucanus cervus*) **1**: *39*

Tortoise beetle (*Chelymorpha cribraria*) **1**: *38, 41*

Tsete fly (*Trypanosoma brucei*) **4**: *223*

Velvet worm (*Aysheaia pedunculata*) **2**: *99*; **6**: *312, 315*; **10**: *603*

Water scorpion (*Ranatra brevicollis*) **2**: *66, 67*

Weaver ant (*Oecophylla smaragdina*) **1**: *12, 12*; **7**: *405*

Boldface numbers before colons indicate volumes; numbers following colons indicate pages; *italic* numbers are the page numbers of illustrations.

Fish

Arapaima/pirarucu (*Arapaima gigas*) **4:** 211; **8:** *448*

Archerfish (*Eutropiellus debauwi*) **4:** 212, *213*

Australian lungfish (*Neoceratodus forsteri*) **4:** 214

Bull shark (*Carcharhinus leucas*) **4:** 211

Curimbata fish (*Prochilodus scrofa*) **1:** 45

Electric eel (*Electrophorus electricus*) **3:** 168; **4:** *212–214;* **10:** *593*

Fire eel (*Mastacembelus erythrotaenia*) **3:** *168*

Glass catfish (*Kryptopterus bicirrhis*) **4:** *212*

Splashing tetra (*Copella arnoldi*) **4:** *213*

Tambaqui (*Colossoma macropomum*) **10:** *584*

Walking catfish (*Clarias batrachus*) **4:** *213*

Reptiles and Amphibians

African clawed toad (*Xenopus laevis*) **1:** *9*

Anaconda (*Eunectes murinus*) **2:** 84; **3:** 130; **7:** *407–408;* **9:** *530*

Black caiman (*Melanosuchus niger*) **3:** *137*

Boa constrictor (*Boa constrictor*) **3:** *130–131;* **4:** *232;* **7:** *407–408;* **9:** *531*

Boyd's forest dragon (*Hypsilurus boydii*) **9:** *490*

Chinese box turtle (*Cuora flavomarginata*) **10:** *589*

Chinese fire-bellied toad (*Bombina orientalis*) **1:** *9*

Dwarf gecko (*Lepidoblepharis heyerorum*) **5:** *255*

Dwarf crocodile (*Osteolaemus tetraspis*) **9:** *491*

Estuarine crocodile (*Crocodylus porosus*) **3:** *135*

Eyelash viper (*Bothrops schegelli*) **5:** *287;* **9:** *491*

Fer-de-lance (*Bothrops asper*) **9:** *492, 493, 531*

Foam nest frog (*Chiromantis xerampelina*) **7:** *404*

Gaboon viper (*Bitis gabonica*) **1:** *5;* **3:** *125;* **9:** *493*

Giant toad (*Bufo marinus*) **4:** *232;* **5:** *249*

Glass frog (*Hyalinobatrachium fleischmanni*) **1:** *9;* **2:** *74;* **10:** *576–577, 577*

Goliath frog (*Conraua goliath*) **1:** *5;* **5:** *248, 248*

Green iguana (*Iguana iguana*) **4:** *232;* **5:** *294, 295,* **6:** *334*

Green tree frog (*Hyla cineria*) **2:** *74*

Green tree python (*Morella viridis*) **3:** *131*

Green vine snake (*Oxybelis fulgidus*) **9:** *532*

Hinge-backed tortoise (*Kinixys erosa*) **9:** *491*

Horned/leaf frog (*Ceratophrys ornata*) **2:** *74*

Indian python (*Python molurus*) **9:** *531, 533*

Jumping viper (*Porthidium nummifer*) **9:** *530*

King cobra (*Ophiophagus hannah*) **1:** 25; **3:** *118–119*

Komodo dragon (*Varanus komodoensis*) **6:** *333*

Leaf-tailed gecko (*Uroplatus fimbriatus*) **5:** *256;* **9:** *491*

Madagascan green day gecko (*Phelsuma madagascariensis*) **5:** *256*

Matamata turtle (*Chelus fimbriatus*) **10:** *587*

Mugger/marsh crocodile (*Crocodylus palustris*) **3:** *135, 137*

Mussurana (*Clelia clelia*) **9:** *531*

New Guinea crocodile (*Crocodylus novaguineae*) **3:** *135, 135*

Panther chameleon (*Furcifer pardalis*) **1:** *42*

Red-eyed leaf frog (*Agalychnis callidryas*) **1:** *9;* **3:** *132;* **5:** *246, 247;* **6:** *336;* **7:** *399*

Reticulated python (*Python reticulates*) **1:** *24;* **9:** *531*

Boldface numbers before colons indicate volumes; numbers following colons indicate pages; *italic* numbers are the page numbers of illustrations.

Scorpion mud turtle
(*Kinosternon scorpioides*)
10: *588*

Smooth-fronted caiman
(*Paleosuchus trigonatus*)
3: *135*, 137

Spectacled caiman (*Caiman crocodilus*) **2**: *85*; **3**: *134*, 136

Surinam toad (*Pipa pipa*) **1**: 9: **5**: 248

Tokay gecko (*Gekko gecko*)
5: 256; **6**: *332*, 333

Turnip-tailed gecko
(*Thecadactylus rapicaudus*)
5: 256

Yellow-footed tortoise
(*Geochelone denticulata*)
4: 181

Boldface numbers before colons indicate volumes; numbers following colons indicate pages; *italic* numbers are the page numbers of illustrations.

Comprehensive Index

acacia 8: 461
Achuar people 9: 538
Africa 1: 2–5, 2, 44–45; 3: 114, 124–125, 129, 141, 146; 4: 181, 189–190, 193, 196
African Timber Organization 1: 5
agoutis 4: 206, 232; 5: 240; 6: 331
agriculturalists 2: 83
Aka people 1: 3; 3: 129; 5: 288
Akha people 5: 277
Alaska 10: 556, 564, 569
alamendro 4: 220
alerce 9: 516
algae 4: 217; 5: 252, 291; 8: 451; 10: 553
alligators 6: 336, 339
Amazon rain forest 2: 94–95, 108–109; 3: 128; 10: 593
Amazon River 1: 6–7, 20; 5: 290–291; 9: 499, 501–502, 499, 518, 522, 537; 10: 597, 600, 604
Amazon River basin 3: 115, 146; 4: 192, 217–218; 6: 344; 7: 376, 378, 380–381, 416; 9: 496–497, 499, 501; 10: 581, 598, 600
Amazonia 1: 2, 6–7, 6, 44; 4: 80, 189, 195, 215; 6: 301; 8: 476–477; 9: 489, 494–495, 497, 518, 535–538
amphibians 1: 7, 8–9; 9: 516, 537; 10: 593 (for species, see individual entries)
Angel, Jimmy 4: 199
Angel Falls (SEE Cherun-Meru)
Angkor Wat 5: 278
anhingas 6: 339
annatto 9: 519
anoas 6: 302–303
anoles 3: 122; 6: 334, 335; 9: 492

ant thrushes 2: 59
antbirds 2: 59; 3: 162
anteaters 1: 13; 4: 207; 6: 308–309; 7: 407; 9: 518; 10: 571
   giant 1: 13
   kinkajou 4: 207
   spiny, or echidna 6: 353
   tree, or tamandua 1: 13, 13; 4: 207
   two-toed, or silky 1: 13, 4: 232; 6: 309, 309
antelopes 1: 14–15
   bongo 1: 14, 15
   duikers 1: 15
   nilgai 7: 390
   pygmy 1: 15
   royal 1: 15
   Suni 3: 160
anthropologists 2: 82
anthuriums 10: 591
ants 1: 10–12; 2: 59, 85; 3: 121, 123, 163; 4: 184, 209, 217, 233; 5: 241, 274; 6: 305, 307, 310, 315; 7: 415; 8: 480; 10: 560, 571, 584
   army, or driver 1: 10–11, 10; 2: 84; 4: 207, 231; 5: 241
   leaf-cutter 1: 11, 11; 3: 162; 5: 252–253; 10: 553, 554
   legionary 1: 11
   weaver 1: 12, 12; 7: 405
antshrikes 10: 595
apes 1: 16–18; 6: 356; 8: 469
Aphelandra 9: 523
aphids 5: 274; 6: 307
Arara people 8: 435
Argentina 4: 180; 9: 535; 10: 550, 552
argus pheasant 3: 122
Ariau River 1: 6

armadillos 1: 19; 4: 207; 6: 309; 7: 407
   giant 1:19
   lesser fairy, or pink fairy 1: 19
   nine-banded 1: 19, 19
aroids 10: 581
arums 4: 219–220
   titan 4: 222
   white arum lilies 3: 124
Ashaninka people 1: 20–21, 20–21
Asia 1: 22–25, 44; 3: 114
Asian fairy bluebird 7: 397
Asmat people 5: 289, 289; 6: 343
Australia 1: 6, 26–27, 26; 3: 115; 4: 189–190, 201; 9: 487; 10: 550–552, 581
Australian honeyeater 4: 205
avocados 2: 61; 4: 225, 229; 5: 251; 9: 520
aye-ayes 1: 4; 4: 206, 206; 6: 348–349, 354; 7: 408
azaleas 10: 558
azobe 1: 3

babirusas 4: 179, 8: 445, 446
baboons 3: 123
bacteria 1: 28, 28; 2: 52; 3: 140–141, 151, 163–164; 4: 205, 233; 5: 240, 273; 7: 415; 9: 508; 10: 553–554, 561, 582
Baka people 3: 125; 5: 279; 8: 437, 437; 9: 517
balsa 10: 575
bamboo 9: 518; 10: 558
bananas 4: 219, 225–226, 225; 5: 251; 8: 454
   plantains 4: 225
bandicoots 1: 27
Bantu people 1: 3
baobab flowers 5: 254

Boldface numbers before colons indicate volumes; **boldface** numbers following colons indicate whole articles; *italic* numbers are the page numbers of illustrations.

barbets 4: 206; 5: 273, 276
bare-necked umbrella bird 2: 99
bats 1: 29–32; 2: 78–79, 84, 96, 100; 4: 177, 207, 221–222; 5: 275–276; 6: 308, 352, 354; 7: 363, 407, 409; 8: 462; 10: 595
   bulldog, or fishing bat 1: 30
   false vampire 1: 30, 2: 100
   fringe-lipped 1: 31
   fruit 1: 4; 9: 518; 10: 551
   Kitti's hog-nosed 1: 30; 6: 352
   leaf-nosed 6: 352
   long-nosed 8: 462
   Queensland tube-nosed 1: 32
   short-tailed fruit 1: 32
   vampire 1: 30; 2: 100; 4: 205
     common 1: 30–31
     hairy-legged 1: 30
     white-winged 1: 30–31
     white tent-building 1: 31, 32; 2: 78
bauhinias 9: 508
bears 1: 33; 2: 87; 4: 232; 5: 276; 6: 355; 9: 516
   black 1: 33; 7: 397, 413; 10: 558, 558
   grizzly 1: 33
   sloth 1: 33, 33
   spectacled 1: 33; 2: 87
   sun 1: 33; 2: 85, 87
beavers 7: 399
beeches 7: 406; 9: 516
   silky 10: 551
bees 4: 205; 7: 403; 8: 461–462
   carpenter 1: 35, 35; 8: 461
   euglossine 4: 222
   honey 1: 35; 8: 461
   stingless 1: 35
bees and wasps 1: 34–36; 5: 275–276; 6: 305, 308, 310, 313, 315, 331 (SEE ALSO wasps)

beetles 1: 37–41, 46–47; 3: 141, 163; 5: 240–241, 273, 275; 6: 305, 310–311, 313; 10: 554, 572, 584
   bombardier 6: 306
   carrion 3: 141; 6: 314
   chafer, Australian 1: 39
   click 1: 37, 47
   dung 3: 141; 5: 241, 241; 6: 307, 314
   fiddle, or violin 1: 39
   fireflies 1: 41, 46–47; 3: 133
   fungus 6: 313
   glowworms 1: 46, 46
   goliath 1: 40
   harlequin 4: 232; 6: 307
   hercules 1: 40
   jewel 1: 41
   long-horned 1: 38
     harlequin 1: 38
   rhinoceros 1: 40–41
     three-horned 1: 40
   stag 1: 39
   tortoise 1: 38, 41
   water 6: 339
Belize 2: 98–99; 3: 129; 10: 569
bellbirds 2: 61, 99
biodiversity 1: 7, 23, 42–45; 3: 164–165; 4: 197; 9: 534–536; 10: 583
bioluminescence 1: 46–47; 4: 224
biomass 2: 52–53
biomes 2: 56
biotechnology 2: 54–55, 54
birches 7: 390
birds, general 1: 43; 2: 56–63; 6: 308, 337–338; 7: 389, 397, 400, 403–404, 410, 412; 5: 240; 9: 536–538; 10: 553, 558, 571, 584, 594–595 (for species, see individual entries)
birds of paradise 2: 62–63, 63, 83; 3: 132
black booyong 10: 551
black-headed caiques 2: 58

bladderworts 1: 28
blood vine 10: 551
blush tulip oak 10: 551
Bohorok River gorge 6: 300
Bolivia 3: 146
boobies 7: 363
Borneo 1: 23, 23, 43; 3: 156–157; 4: 177–178, 196; 6: 300–301, 343; 7: 376; 9: 495, 497
botanists 2: 82–83
bowerbirds 2: 62; 3: 132; 7: 399
   satin 2: 62
Boyd's forest dragon 9: 490
Brahmaputra River 4: 217
Brazil 1: 6, 44; 2: 94–95, 109; 3: 146–147, 151; 4: 180, 195–196; 5: 291; 6: 344; 9: 535–536, 538; 10: 550, 552, 604–605
Brazil nut trees 3: 170
Brazil nuts 4: 196, 206, 230
breadfruit 4: 228; 5: 251, 251
broadbills 10: 595
bromeliads 1: 8; 2: 59, 64, 64, 69, 78–79, 89, 99–100; 3: 120, 139, 155, 162; 4: 183–184, 183; 7: 391; 8: 451, 478; 9: 507, 513; 10: 571, 576, 581, 599
   tank 4: 202
bugs 2: 65–68; 4: 205; 6: 310–311, 313, 315
   anatomy 2: 65–68
   aquatic 2: 65–67
   assassin 2: 68
     African 2: 68, 68
   backswimmers 2: 66
   defense 2: 66
   feeding 4: 205
   giant water bugs 2: 67, 67
   life cycle 2: 65–66
   peanut 7: 401, 402
   rhodnius 2: 68
   shield 6: 315, 315
   stinkbugs 2: 66
   water boatmen 2: 65, 66

Boldface numbers before colons indicate volumes; boldface numbers following colons indicate whole articles; *italic* numbers are the page numbers of illustrations.

water scorpions **2:** 66–67, *66*

water stick insects **2:** 67

water striders **2:** 68

Burma (SEE Myanmar)

bush babies (SEE Galagos)

bush meat **2:** 105; **3:** 125; **4:** 181

bushdogs **2:** 86, *86*

butterflies **1:** 7; **3:** 123; **9:** 536–538; **10:** 557–558, 591 (SEE ALSO butterflies and moths)

bird wings **2:** 70, *70*

Queen Alexandra's **2:** 70, *70*; **6:** 310

bluebottle swallowtails **2:** *71*

glass-wings **2:** 71

heliconiids **2:** *69*, 70; **4:** *232*; **6:** 306–307; **8:** 452

Isabella tiger **6:** 315

leaf **2:** 71

Madagascan red-and-gold skipper **4:** *177*

morphos **2:** 72, *72*; **6:** *304*

blue morpho **10:** 552

nymphalids **6:** 306

owl **2:** 73

Phyciodes philyra **6:** 315

butterflies and moths **2:** 69–73; **4:** 205; **5:** 275; **6:** 304–307, *304*, 310, *311*, 313, 315, 330–331; **8:** 461

defenses **2:** 71–75

life cycle **2:** 69–70, 79

poisonous **2:** 69–70, 72

puddling **2:** 71, *71*

species of butterflies (SEE butterflies)

species of moths (SEE moths)

buttress roots **3:** 170, *170*; **9:** 507, 509, *509*; **10:** 573, *573*

caboclos **4:** 215, *215*

cacao **2:** 55, *55*; **4:** 219, 228–229, *229*; **10:** 585

cacti **10:** 581

caecilians **1:** 8, *8*; **10:** 593

caimans (SEE crocodilians)

Cambodia **4:** 189; **6:** 343

Cameroon **1:** 3, 5; **6:** 343; **9:** 517; **10:** 581

camouflage **2:** 71–72, **74–75**, 84, 91, 102; **3:** 131; **5:** 270; **6:** 315, 335; **7:** 364–365, 402; **9:** 491–493, 527, 529, 532, 542–543; **10:** 555, 576–577

Canada **9:** 515; **10:** 556

canopy **2:** 56, 61, 66, 71, **76–79**, *76–78*, 100; **3:** 116–117, 124, 129, 153, 165, 167, 170–171; **4:** 198–200; **8:** 450, 477; **10:** 551–552, 570–572, 583–584, 597–598

researching the **2:** 76–77

capybaras **4:** *232*; **5:** 275; **6:** 339, 353, 355; **9:** 503–506, *504*, 536–537

caracaras **10:** 554

carbon cycle **2:** **80–81**, *80*; **5:** 261–263

carbon dioxide **2:** 80–81; **3:** 115, 148

careers **2:** **82–83**

carnivores **2:** **84–87**, 90–93, 100, 104; **3:** 167; **4:** 206–207, *232*; **6:** 354

carnivorous plants **2:** **88–89**, *88–89*; **7:** 415; **8:** 449, 451

bladderworts **2:** 89

bog violets **2:** 89

pitchers (SEE pitcher plants)

sundews **2:** 88–89, *89*

Caroni swamp, Trinidad **7:** 363

casaurina **7:** 390

cassava, or manioc **4:** 230; **9:** 510

cassowaries **1:** 27; **2:** 57, *57*; **3:** 122; **10:** 594

caterpillars **3:** 121; **4:** 204, 207; **5:** 274, *275*; **6:** 311, 313, 315

cats **2:** 85–86, **90–93**, 100; **3:** 123, 133; **6:** 356; **7:** 409–410; **9:** 518; **10:** 595

African golden **2:** 93

fishing **2:** *90*, 93

flat-headed **2:** 93

iriomote **2:** 92

jaguars (SEE jaguars)

jaguarundis (SEE jaguarundis)

leopards (SEE leopards)

marbled **2:** 93

margays **2:** 93, *93*, 100

ocelots **2:** 93, 100

tigers (SEE tigers)

cattle ranching **2:** **94–95**, *94*, 100, 108–109; **3:** 147; **4:** 180, 187, 195; **6:** 343; **7:** 380; **9:** 497, 538

cave swiftlets **2:** 96

caves **2:** 96, *96*

ceiba (capok, kapok, or silk cotton) **3:** 170–171; **6:** 331; **8:** 453

cellulose **3:** 140

centipedes **2:** 97; **4:** 207, 217; **5:** 241; **6:** 315; **10:** 572

scolopendra **2:** 97, *97*

Central African Republic **1:** 3, 5; **3:** 129

Central America **1:** 43–44; **2:** 63, 94, **98–101**, *98*; **4:** 179–180, 189; **9:** 487, 536; **10:** 581

chameleons **1:** 4, 45; **2:** 75, 85, 102, *102*; **4:** 204, 207, *207*; **6:** 309, 333–334; **9:** 491

panther **1:** *42*

Parson's **1:** *42*

Cherun-Meru, or Angel Falls **4:** 199

Boldface numbers before colons indicate volumes; boldface numbers following colons indicate whole articles; *italic* numbers are the page numbers of illustrations.

chestnut 7: 390

chevrotains 5: *275*
    water 1: 5

chicle 9: 517

Chile 9: 515, 535; **10**: 556

chimpanzees 1: 2, 4, 16–17, *17*;
    2: 103–105; 3: 125, 129,
    165; 4: 193, 231; **6**: 337;
    7: 399, 405
    bonobo 1: 17, 45;
      2: 103–105, *104*
    common 2: *103*

China 1: 22; **10**: 550, 558

Chiricoa people 5: 289;
    7: 376

cholera 1: 28

cicadas 2: **106**, *106*; 3: 121–122,
    133; **6**: 304, *308*

cinchona 4: 196; 7: 373

cinnamon tree 7: 390

civets 2: 87, **107**
    palm 2: 87, *107*

clear-cutting 2: **108–109**, *108*;
    5: 242; **6**: *340*, 341–342,
    344; 7: 411; 8: 472

climate and weather
    3: **114–115**; 4: 189–192,
    198, 200, 202; 5: 284–285

climate, forest 3: 114–115, 124,
    162, 164–165; 8: 474–478;
    9: 515–518; **10**: 550,
    556–557, 580–581

climate, world 2: 80–81; 3: 115;
    9: 487, 515

climbers 3: **116–117**, 165;
    8: 449–451
    Marantia 8: *450*
    passionflowers 8: *449*, 452
    peperomias 8: *450*

cloud forests 1: 2; 2: 99; 8: 478,
    478

coatis 2: 87, 100; 3: 165; **6**: 355,
    355

cobras 3: **118–119**, *118–119*

cockatoos 5: 276
    Moluccan 8: 433
    salmon-crested 8: *432*
    slender-billed 8: 433

cockroaches 2: 96; **3**: **120**;
    4: 233; 5: 240; 7: 407,
    409
    giant tropical 3: 120
    Madagascan hissing
      3: *120*
    wood roaches 3: 120

cocks-of-the-rock 3: 132
    4: 232

cocoa 8: 454 (SEE ALSO cacao)

coffee 4: 226, 227; 8: 454

Colombia 2: 94, 99; 3: 146;
    7: 417; 9: 534–536

communication 3: **121–123**

Congo 3: **124–125**, 146; 4: 181,
    199

Congo, Democratic Republic
    of the 1: 3, 5; **6**: 343

Congo peafowl 1: 4

Congo Republic 1: 3

Congo River 7: 370;
    9: 501–502, *502*

Congo River basin 1: 3–5, 45;
    10: 581

conifers 7: 412–413

conservation 1: 5; 2: 99, 101;
    3: **126–129**, 141; 4: 197;
    5: 242, 283; 9: 487–488

Convention on International
    Trade in Endangered
    Species of Wild Fauna and
    Flora (CITES) 9: 529

copepod 3: 138, *138*

cormorants 7: 363

Costa Rica 1: 44; 2: 94, 98–99
    98; 3: 129; **10**: 568

cougar, or mountain lion
    7: 412–413

courtship 3: **132–133**

crabs 3: 138–139, 141, 163;
    10: 599
    coconut 3: 138; 5: 273
    hermit 3: 138
    land 4: 233
      Caribbean land 3: 139
      red land 3: *139*
    robber **6**: *313*

crayfish, blue mountain **10**: 551

crested honeycreepers **10**: 559

Cretaceous period 4: 190, 202,
    208

crickets 3: 121–122, *121*;
    5: 267–270; 7: 408
    bush 2: 75
    brachytrupes membranaceus
      5: 269
    cave 2: 75
    rhicnogryllus lepidus 5: 269
    wetas 7: 406

crocodilians 3: **134–137**; 4: 206,
    232; 7: 405, 408;
    9: 490–491, 502; **10**: 594
    caimans 2: 84–85;
      3: 134–137
      black 3: 137
      dwarf, or smooth-fronted
        3: *135*, 137
      spectacled 2: *85*; 3: *134*,
        136
    crocodiles 2: 84–85, *85*
      dwarf crocodiles 9: *491*
      Johnston's, or freshwater
        3: *135*, 136
      mugger, or marsh
        3: *135*, *137*
      New Guinea 3: 135, *135*
      saltwater, or estuarine
        3: *135*, *135*
      West African dwarf
        3: 135

crowned wood partridges 8: 445

crow's ash **10**: 551

crustaceans 3: **138–139**; **6**: 310,
    314
    crabs (SEE crabs)
    prawns 7: 363
    shrimps 3: 138; 7: 363
    wood lice 3: 138–139

curare 7: 375, 8: 439–440

curassows 3: 133

cuscuses **6**: 301

cycads 9: 508

dams (SEE ALSO
    hydroelectricity)
    3: **147–148**, 151–152;

Boldface numbers before colons indicate volumes; **boldface** numbers following colons indicate whole articles; *italic* numbers are the page numbers of illustrations.

5: 290–291

Turucui dam **5**: *291*

darters **4**: 207; **6**: 338

Darwin, Charles **7**: 402, *402*

decomposers **3**: **140–141**, 166;
4: 223, 233; **5**: 252, 285;
6: 307, 315; **7**: 415;
10: 557, 561, 582, 596, 603

decomposition **2**: 81

deer **1**: 25, 28; **2**: 75; **3**: 123,
142–145; **4**: 204–205;
5: 273; **6**: 302, 355–356;
7: 363, 407–408; **9**: 526;
10: 553

axis, or chital **1**: 25; **3**: 143,
143; **7**: 363

black-tailed **7**: 413

lesser mouse **6**: 302

muntjac **3**: 142, 145, *145*

red brocket **3**: 144–145,
144

rusa **6**: 302

sambar **1**: 25; **3**: *142*, 145;
7: 390; **9**: *517*

spotted **7**: 390

Visayan spotted **3**: 145

deforestation **2**: 52–53, 55,
80–81, 94–95, 108–109;
3: 125, **146–149**, 171;
4: 176–178, 180–182, 185,
187, 194–195, 203;
5: 238–239, 260–263, 285;
6: 301, 340–345, 348–349;
7: 363, *363*, 380;
9: 486–489, 496, 536, 538;
10: 559, 581, 583

Derris **9**: 507, 510

Dinizia excelsa **3**: 170

dinosaurs **4**: *192–193*, 202–203

dipterocarps **1**: 24; **3**: 171, *171*;
4: 187; **9**: *519*; **10**: 573–574,
574

diseases **2**: 54–55, 65, 68;
3: **150–151**; **6**: 317–318,
320, 322; **7**: 372–375,
378–379, 381, 391;
8: 430–431, 435;
9: 495–496, 503, 506

malaria **3**: 150–151

onchocerciasis, or river
blindness **3**: 150–151

Schistosomiasis, or
bilharziasis **3**: 150–151;
8: 430–431

yellow fever **3**: 150–151

dolphins, river **3**: **152**; **4**: 232;
9: 502, 518; **10**: 595

botos **3**: 152, *152*

susus **3**: 152

dormancy **3**: 153; **9**: 519;
10: 574

Douglas fir **7**: 412; **10**: 557

dragonflies and damselflies
3: **154–155**; **6**: 305, *305*;
10: 599

aeshnid **3**: 154

giant damselfly **3**: 155, *155*

drills **4**: 181

ducks **7**: 412

dugongs (SEE manatees)

dumbcanes, or diffenbachias
10: 591

durian **5**: 251; **9**: 520–521

Dyak people **3**: **156–157**,
156–157; **4**: *197*; **5**: 280,
288–289; **8**: *442*; **9**: 495

eagles **2**: 56, 60; **3**: **158–161**,
163; **4**: 207; **7**: 403, 412;
10: 594

crowned **2**: 60; **3**: 158–161,
158–159, 165; **7**: 403

harpy **2**: 60, 79;
3: 158–161, *161*; **4**: 232

Philippine, or
monkey-eating **2**: 60;
4: 177; **3**: 158–161, *160*;
5: 282

ebony **1**: 4; **3**: 124, 146; **8**: 459;
10: 575

ecological niches **2**: 56; **3**: 165;
4: 193

ecology **3**: **162–163**

ecosystems **3**: **164–167**; **4**: 191,
231; **9**: 486–487; **10**: 553,
558, 582

ecotourism (SEE tourism)

Ecuador **2**: 101; **3**: 146; **9**: 488,
535, 537–538

eels **3**: **168**

electric **3**: 168; **4**: 212–214;
10: 593

fire **3**: 168, *168*

spiny **3**: 168

swamp **3**: 168; **4**: 213–214

Efe people **3**: 125

egrets **7**: 363

elephants **3**: **169**; **4**: 204; **5**: 274,
6: 352, 355; **10**: 583

African **3**: 125, 129, 169;
4: 201; **6**: 331

Asian, **1**: 25; **3**: 169, *169*;
5: *274*; **6**: 303; **7**: 390,
397; **10**: *568*

elk **7**: 399, 413, **10**: 558

Roosevelt elk **7**: *413*

emergents **3**: 165, **170–171**;
10: 572, *573*

endangered species **1**: 5, 7, 45;
2: 63, 86–87, 92;
3: 126–129, 135–136, 145,
161; **4**: **176–182**;
6: 348–349; **9**: 498, 529,
536; **10**: 563

epiphylls **8**: 451, *451*; **9**: 524,
524; **10**: 583

epiphytes **2**: 64, 78, 99–100;
3: 117, 120; **4**: **183–184**,
183–184, 189; **6**: 328;
7: 393; **8**: 424–425,
424–425, 444, 449, 476,
478; **9**: 507–508, 510;
10: 551–552, 576, 581, 585,
599

Equatorial Guinea **1**: 3

erosion **4**: **185–188**, *185–186*;
5: 242; **6**: 341, 348; **7**: 380;
10: 599, 601

ethnobotanists **3**: 157

eucalyptus **1**: 27; **4**: 188, *188*;
8: 455; **9**: 496; **10**: 571,
571, 575

Eungella honeyeater **1**: 27

evolution **4**: 191–193, 202

Boldface numbers before colons indicate volumes; **boldface** numbers following colons indicate whole articles; *italic* numbers are the page numbers of illustrations.

evolution of the rain forest
   4: 189–193
exploitation 4: 194–197
exploration and research
   4: 198–201
extinction 1: 45; 2: 63, 99;
   3: 146–148; 4: 176–178,
   181, 202–203; 8: 458;
   9: 498, 536; 10: 563

farming 1: 4–5, 7; 2: 53, 55, 83,
   94–95, 100, 105; 3: 125,
   128–129, 147–148;
   5: 244–245, 262, 282–283,
   292–293; 6: 301, 322;
   9: 486–487, 494–495,
   494, 525–526, *526*;
   10: 575
Fauna and Flora Preservation
   Society 4: 201
feeding 4: 204–207
ferns 2: 100; 4: 183–184, 191,
   208–209; 5: 240; 7: 412;
   8: 451–453; 9: 508, 523;
   10: 553, 571, 581, 599
   adder's-tongue 4: 209
   bird's nest 3: 162; 4: 209;
      10: 551
   bracket 4: 209
   coral 4: *209*
   elephant 4: 208
   hare's foot 4: 209
   potato 4: 209
   ribbon 4: 209
   staghorn 4: *208*, 209
figs 3: 165, *165*; 4: 232; 5: 251;
   10: 580
Fiji 4: 189
finches 2: 58; 4: 206; 5: 273,
   276
fireflies (SEE beetles)
fish 3: 123; 4: 210–214,
   215–218; 6: 308; 7: 363,
   376, 408; 9: 499,
   501–502, 518, 522;
   10: 585, 592–593
   arapaimas (SEE pirarucus)
   archerfish 4: 212, *213*

arowhanas 4: 211, *211*
bull sharks 4: 211
butterfly 4: 213
catfish 4: 211, 213
   glass 4: 212, *212*
   walking 4: 213
cichlids 4: 212
curimbata 1: *45*
eels (SEE eels)
electric rays 4: 212
elephant 4: 210
guppies 4: 212; 10: 593
   four-eyed fish 4: 212
hatchet 4: 213
jaracui 4: 218
leaf 4: 211
lungfish 4: 210, 214
mudskippers 4: 210, 213;
   7: 363, **394**, *394*;
   10: *592*
paradise 7: 403
piranhas (SEE piranhas)
pirarucus (SEE pirarucus)
salmon 7: 412; 8: 471–472
saw 4: 211
stingrays 10: 593
swordtail characin 4: 212
tambaqui 9: 518; 10: *584*
tetras
   neon 4: 210, *210*;
      10: 593
   splashing 4: 213
fishing 4: **215–216**, *215–216*;
   9: 502, 510
flame-of-the-forest 7: 390, *390*
fleas 6: 304, 336
flies 3: 141; 4: **223–224**, 233;
   6: 307; 8: 461, 473
   botflies 4: 223–224
   fungus 6: 313
   New Zealand glowworm, or
      fungus gnat 1: 47;
      4: 224, *224*
   pantophthalmid 4: 223;
      6: 307, 313
   robber 4: 224; 6: *306*,
      307
   tsetse 4: 223, *223*

flooding 4: 214, **217–218**,
   217–218; 7: 376; 9: 499,
   501–502, 518, *518*, 522;
   10: 585, 598–601
flowering plants 4: 189–193,
   219–222 (for species, see
   individual entries)
flycatchers 2: 58–59; 3: 125;
   6: 308
food chains 2: 52–53, 56, 60,
   81, 84, 90, 92; 5: 273;
   6: 315; 10: 553
food web 4: **231–233**; 6: 354
foods 4: **225–230**; 9: 510, 518
forest fires 2: 95, *95*;
   5: 238–239, *238–239*, 243
forest floor 2: 76–77, 99–100;
   3: 165; 5: **240–241**, *240*,
   244, 253; 9: 523–524;
   10: 572
forestry 2: 83, 5: **242–245**
   agroforestry 5: 244–245,
      244
   artificial regeneration
      5: 244
   natural regeneration
      5: 243–244
   seed orchards 5: 245
   selective felling 5: 242–243
foxes 4: 232; 7: 409
   gray 2: 86
French Guiana 4: *200*
friagem 4: 215
Friends of the Earth 4: 201
frigates 7: 363
frogs 2: 64, 74, 89; 3: 121,
   132–133, 163; 7: 408;
   10: 571, *592*, 593–594,
   598–599
   American nest-building
      1: 9
   common mantella 1: 43
   flying 5: 249; 6: 338
   foam nest 7: 404
   gastric brooding 1: 27
   glass 1: 9; 2: 74;
      10: 576–577, *577*
   golden 1: *43*

Boldface numbers before colons indicate volumes; **boldface** numbers following colons indicate whole articles; *italic* numbers are the page numbers of illustrations.

goliath **1**: 5; **5**: 248, *248*
leaf **10**: 576–577
Malaysian horned **2**: *74*
    5: 248–249
marsupial **10**: 577
poison dart **1**: 9;
    5: 246–248, *247*; **8**: 457;
    10: 576–577, *576*
psyllophryne didactyla
    5: 247
pygmy marsupial **1**: 9
red-eyed leaf **1**: 9; **3**: *132*;
    5: *246, 247*; **6**: *336*;
    7: 399
reed **10**: 577
Sarayacu **1**: 7, *7*
tree **1**: 4, 8–9; **2**: *74, 79*;
    5: 246, 249; **6**: *336*;
    10: **576–577**, 593
whistling **5**: 248
frogs and toads **1**: 8–9;
    5: **246–249**; **6**: 308,
    336–337, 339; **9**: 502
camouflage **5**: 249
poisonous **5**: 246–247, 249
reproduction **5**: 247–249
toads (SEE toads)
fruit **3**: 117; **5**: **250–251**,
    275–276; **9**: 521; **10**: 575,
    585 (for species, see
    individual entries)
fungi **1**: 46–47, *47*; **2**: 52, 96;
    3: 140–141, *141*,
    162–164; **4**: 233;
    5: 240–241, **252–253**,
    285; **7**: 415; **8**: 451;
    9: 487, 507–508; **10**: 549,
    553–554, *553*, 561, 572,
    582
candle snuff **5**: 253
cookeina **5**: *252*, 253
inky caps **5**: 253
maiden's veil stinkhorn
    5: 253, *253*
marasmius **5**: 253
Phillipsia cup **5**: 241
puff balls **5**: 253
fungus gardens **5**: 252–253

Gabon **1**: 3; **6**: 343
galagos **3**: 123; **5**: 254, *254*,
    274; **7**: 408; **8**: 468
game wardens **2**: 83
gaurs **4**: *176*; **7**: 390
geckos **5**: **255–256**; **6**: 332–336
    dwarf **5**: 255
    flying **5**: 255, *255*
    green day **5**: 256, *256*
    leaf-tailed **5**: 256
        Madagascan leaf-tailed
        9: *490, 491*
    naked-fingered **5**: 256
    tokay **5**: 256; **6**: *332, 333*
    turnip-tailed **5**: 256
gedu nohor **1**: 3
geese **7**: 412
genetic engineering **2**: 54–55
genets **6**: 354, *354*
gewa **7**: 362
giant Amazon water lily **4**: 217,
    219, 221, *221*; **8**: 453, *453*
giant otters **4**: 181; **5**: 257, *257*
giant redwoods **10**: 557, *557*
giant stinging tree **6**: 324, *324*;
    10: 583
gibbons **1**: 17–18; **3**: *117*;
    5: **258–259**, *259*; **6**: 337;
    8: *470*
    hoolock **10**: 551
    Kloss's **5**: 259
    siamang **1**: 18, *18*; **5**: 258,
    258
gingers **4**: 219–221, *219*; **9**: 524
    10: 591
ginkgo **10**: 558
global warming **2**: 81; **3**: 115,
    148; **5**: **260–263**, 282, 291;
    8: 464, 477; **9**: 487
Gondwana **4**: 189–190
goran **7**: 362
gorillas **1**: 4, 16–17; **3**: 124, 129;
    4: 193; **5**: **264–266**;
    6: 356; **7**: 405; **8**: 458
    eastern lowland **3**: 125,
    125; **5**: 264, *265*
    mountain **1**: 16, 45; **4**: *182*;
    5: 264, *264*; **7**: *405*

    western lowland **1**: *16*;
    5: 264; **7**: 399
granadilla **4**: 229
Grand Carajas Program **7**: 381
grasshoppers **3**: 122; **4**: 204;
    6: 307, 313
    chlorotypus **5**: 268
    proscopia **5**: 268
    short-winged **5**: 268
    zonoceros **5**: 269
grasshoppers, crickets, and
    katydids **5**: **267–270**;
    6: 305
    (SEE ALSO crickets)
    (SEE ALSO grasshoppers)
    (SEE ALSO katydids)
grebes **6**: 338
greenheart **10**: 575
greenhouse effect **5**: 260–261
Guahibo people **5**: 289; **7**: 376
Guatemala **2**: 94, 98–99; **4**: 218
guavas **4**: 225
Guinea **10**: 581
Guyana **8**: 477

Halmahera **6**: 300
Hawaii **10**: 558–559, *559*
hawks **2**: 60; **4**: 207; **7**: 403;
    10: 594
heliconia, or crab claws **10**: 591,
    591
herbivores **3**: 166–167;
    4: 204–206, 232;
    5: **273–276**; **6**: 354–355
herbs **5**: 271 (SEE ALSO herbs
    and spices)
    lemongrass **5**: 271
    sweet basil **5**: 271
herbs and spices **5**: **271–272**
herons **4**: 207; **7**: 412
hibiscus **4**: 221
hippopotamuses, pygmy **1**: 4
hogs **2**: 75; **4**: 233; **5**: 276
Hoh rain forest **8**: 475
homes **5**: **277–281**, *277–281*,
    293
Honduras **2**: 94, 98–99
honey **8**: 436; **10**: 554

Boldface numbers before colons indicate volumes; **boldface** numbers following colons indicate whole articles; *italic* numbers are the page numbers of illustrations.

honey possums (SEE possums)
honeyguides 8: 436; 10: 554
hoop pines 10: 551
hornbills 1: 4; 3: 125; 4: 178; 10: 571
hot-lips 4: 220; 9: 524; 10: 591
Huaorani people 7: 417
human interference 5: 282–283
humidity 3: 114–115, 162; 4: 176, 200; 5: 284–285
hummingbirds 2: 56–57; 4: 205, 221; 5: 273, 275, 286–287; 6: 331, 337; 7: 376, 404; 8: 460, 460, 462, 478; 10: 557, 591
bee 5: 286
giant 5: 286
ruby-topaz 5: 287
saber-wing 2: 56
stripe-tailed 5: 287
violet-eared 5: 286
humus 10: 557, 582
hunter-gatherers 3: 125, 129; 5: 278–279, 283, 288–289; 8: 435–437, 458
hunting 4: 178, 181–182, 197, 203; 9: 495
hurus 9: 522
hydroelectric dams 7: 380–381
hydroelectricity 6: 320; 7: 380–381; 9: 497, 502, 538; 10: 601
hydrologists 2: 82

Iban people 3: 156; 4: 196; 9: 497
Ibo people 5: 292–293, 292–293
igapo forest 1: 6, 7; 4: 218; 10: 570, 585
Iguaçu Falls 9: 535; 10: 552, 552
iguanas 2: 100; 3: 165; 5: 294–295; 6: 332, 334–335
basilisks 5: 295, 295; 6: 335–336
green, or common 4: 232; 5: 294–295, 294; 6: 334

India 1: 22; 4: 195, 217; 6: 342; 7: 389; 10: 551, 581
Indian rosewood 7: 390
Indochina 4: 189
Indonesia 1: 22–23, 45; 2: 95; 4: 177, 189, 195; 5: 238; 6: 300–303, 343–344; 7: 416; 9: 495, 497; 10: 569, 581
indris (SEE lemurs)
Indus River 4: 217
insectivores 4: 207; 6: 308–309
insects 6: 304–307, 310, 338–339; 9: 526; 10: 581, 583–584 (for species, see individual entries)
International Tropical Timber Organization (ITTO) 1: 5; 6: 341
Intsia 9: *509*
invertebrates, general 6: 310–315; 7: 410 (for species, see individual entries)
iroko (African teak) 1: 4; 3: 125, 146, 171; 4: 195
Ituri forest 10: 581
Ivory Coast 3: 146; 10: 581, 599

jacamars 10: 595
jacanas 8: 453
Jack-in-the-pulpit 10: 591
Jacobson's organs 6: 333
jaguars 2: 85, 86, 90–91, 91, 92, 100; 4: 232–233; 6: 316, 316; 7: 408;
jaguarundis 2: 86, 92, 93
Japan 10: 558
Jatun Sacha Biological Station 9: 488, 537
Java 6: 300–301
jewel thrushes 5: 241

Kaluli people 6: 317–318; 8: 441
kangaroos
muskrat 1: 27
tree 10: 578–579, 578–579

Kapawi Lodge and Ecological Reserve 9: 538
katydids 2: 75; 4: 204; 5: 267–270, 267, 270; 6: 313, 315
lichen 5: 269, 269
mimetica incisa 5: 270
zabalius apicalis 5: 270
Kayapo people 4: 196; 6: 319–320, 319–320
Kenyir, Lake 10: 569
keystone species 3: 165; 4: 233
Kinabalu, Mount 1: 23, 23, 46
kingfishers 7: 412
Javan 6: 303, 303
kiwis 6: 339, 339; 7: 406; 10: 594
klinki pines 3: 170–171
kola 4: 230
Korea 10: 558
Kuna people 6: 321–322, 321–322; 7: 396

Laos 1: 22; 4: 189
laurels 10: 558
leaves 6: 323–324, 323; 8: 443–444, 449–453; 10: 572, 583–584, 598
leeches 4: 205–206; 6: 310, 312, 325, 325, 336–337; 7: 389; 10: 598, 603
lemurs 1: 4, 42; 4: 182, 190; 6: 326–327, 348–349; 8: 455, 468, 468; 10: 595
aye-ayes (SEE aye-ayes)
black 6: 326, 327
brown 1: 42
gentle 6: 327, 327
golden bamboo 4: 176
indris 1: 4, 42; 3: 147; 6: 326–327, 348; 4: 182
red-bellied 1: 43
red-fronted 1: 43
red-ruffed 6: 349, 349
rufous mouse 8: 468–469
sifakas 3: 163; 6: 327, 337
diademed 1: 42; 4: 182
sportive 6: 327

Boldface numbers before colons indicate volumes; **boldface** numbers following colons indicate whole articles; *italic* numbers are the page numbers of illustrations.

leopards **1**: 25; **2**: 90–92; **3**: 133; **7**: 363, 390, 408
    clouded **2**: 93; **8**: *457*
leukemia **7**: 375
lianas **3**: 116–117, 121, 165; **4**: 196, 215, 221; **8**: 449, 451, *452*; **9**: 520–522; **10**: 571, 581, 590
    Alsomitra **9**: 522
    Macrozanonia macrocarpa **9**: 522
lichens **5**: 252; **6**: **328–329**, *328–329*; **7**: 412; **8**: 449, 451, 478; **10**: 553, 571
    Parmelia **6**: 329
    Strigula **6**: 329
    Usnea **6**: 329
light gaps **3**: 153; **5**: 240; **6**: **330–331**; **10**: 591
limes **4**: 228
liverworts (SEE mosses)
lizards **3**: *122*, 123, 141; **4**: 206; **6**: 308–309, **332–335**, 336; **9**: 490–492, *490*, 518; **10**: 571, 594
    anoles (SEE anoles)
    chisel-teeth **9**: 492
    flying **1**: 24; **6**: 338, *338*
    geckos (SEE geckos)
    iguanas (SEE iguanas)
    Komodo dragons **6**: 333, *333*
    monitors **6**: 332, 334–335
    nose-horned **9**: 491
    skinks (SEE skinks)
    worm **6**: 335, *335*
locomotion **6**: **336–339**
logging **1**: 3–5; **2**: 100, 105, 108–109, *109*; **3**: 125, 129, 147, 149, 157; **4**: 178, 181, 194–195, 201; **5**: 282; **6**: 301, **340–345**; **7**: 379–380; **8**: 455, 463; **9**: 496, 538; **10**: 559, 565, 575, 599
lories (SEE parrots)
lorikeets (SEE parrots)
lorises **6**: 346; **7**: 408; **8**: 468

slender **6**: 346
slow **7**: *408*

Macadamia **4**: 228
macaws **2**: 56, 62–63; **4**: 206; **5**: 241, 276; **7**: 400; **9**: 518, 522; **10**: 571
    military **10**: 593
    scarlet **4**: *232*
Machiguenga people **9**: 495
Mackay tulip oak **1**: 27
Madagascar **1**: 3–4, 42–43, 45; **2**: 102; **3**: 146–147; **4**: 182, *185*, 190; **6**: **347–349**, *347–348*; **8**: 455; **9**: 526, *526*; **10**: 550, 581
magnolia **7**: 390; **10**: 558
mahoganies **1**: 3; **4**: 180–181, 194; **6**: 331, 340; **7**: 390; **8**: 459; **9**: 488, 522; **10**: 575
Makah people **6**: **350–351**, *350–351*
malaria **4**: 200; **7**: 373, 391
Malayan Nature Society **4**: 201
Malaysia **1**: 23; **3**: *147*; **4**: 189, 195; **6**: 343; **9**: 496–497
maleo **2**: 60, *60*; **4**: 179
mammals, general **4**: 203–204, 206; **6**: 336, **352–356**; **7**: 410; **10**: 595 (for species, see individual entries)
manakins **10**: *594*, 595
manatees **6**: 357, *357*; **9**: 502, 518; **10**: 595
    Amazonian **4**: 181
mango **4**: 227–228; **9**: 520
mangosteen **4**: 227
mangrove forest **7**: **362–363**, *362*, 394; **9**: 508–510, *510*, *522*; **10**: 575
mantises **2**: 75; **3**: 133, *133*; **4**: 207; **6**: 308, 311, 315; **7**: **364–365**, *364–365*
    Archimantis **7**: 364
    Asian flower **2**: 75
marmosets and tamarins **5**: 274; **7**: **366–367**, 387; **8**: 469
    buffy-headed marmoset

    4: 180–181; **9**: 536
    common marmosets **7**: 366
    emperor tamarin **7**: 367, *367*
    golden lion tamarin **4**: 180, *180*; **7**: 367; **9**: 536
    pygmy marmoset **7**: *366*
    saddle-back tamarin **7**: 367
marsupials **6**: 301, 309, 338, 353–354; **10**: 595
Maya people **2**: 61; **7**: **368–369**, *368–369*; **9**: 526
Mbuti people **1**: 3, *3*; **3**: 125, 149; **5**: 279, *279*, 288; **7**: **370–371**, *370–371*; **8**: 436–437, *436*
medicinal plants **3**: 148, 151, 157; **4**: 196–197; **7**: **372–375**; **10**: 565, 575
    quinine **3**: 151
medicines **2**: 54–55, 101
megapodes **2**: 60
Mende people **4**: 216
meteorologists **2**: 82
Mexico **2**: 99; **3**: 146; **4**: 180
mice (SEE rodents)
microorganisms **2**: 54–55; **6**: 314; **10**: 553–554, 561
migration **4**: 214, 218; **7**: 376; **9**: 489, 516; **10**: 557
millipedes **3**: 140–141; **4**: 217; **5**: 240; **6**: 310–311, 314; **7**: 377, *377*; **10**: 572
    giant pill **3**: *140*
mimicry **10**: 581, *581*
Mineracao Rio do Norte **7**: 381
mining **1**: 7; **3**: 129, 148, 151–152; **4**: 195; **5**: 282; **6**: 301; **7**: **378–381**, *378–381*; **8**: 463, 465; **9**: 487, *495*, 496–497, 538; **10**: 605
mink **7**: 412
Miskito people **7**: **382–383**, *382–383*; **9**: *496*
mollusks **6**: 312
mongooses **7**: **384**, 409; **10**: 551
    crab-eating **7**: 384

Boldface numbers before colons indicate volumes; **boldface** numbers following colons indicate whole articles; *italic* numbers are the page numbers of illustrations.

mongooses (cont.)
  ring-tailed 7: 384, *384*
  stripe-necked 7: 384
monkeys 2: 77, 79, 100; 3: 116,
  121–123, 133; 4: 181,
  201, 204, 221, 232;
  5: 273, 276; 6: 353,
  355–356; 7: **385–388**;
  8: 469; 9: 518, 536, 538;
  10: 552, 571, 584
  capuchins 4: *232*; 7: 385
  colobus 3: 165; 7: 385–386
    black 7: 387
    black-and-white 7: 398
    Kenyan 7: *388*
    red 1: *4*; 5: *273*; 7: 387,
      398
  DeBrazza's 7: 385
  douroucouli, or night
    monkey 7: 388, *407, 408*
  guenons 7: 386–387
  howler 2: 79; 3: 123,
    123; 7: 386–387
  langur 1: 25; 3: 143, *143*;
    7: *385*, 386
  leaf 1: 25; 7: 386
  macaque 1: 25; 6: 302;
    7: 386
    black 4: 177
    bonnet 7: 390
    lion-tailed 1: 25
    long-tailed 6: 301
    pig-tailed 1: 25; 7: 385
    stump-tailed 7: 390
    toque 1: 25
  mandrills 7: 386–387, *387*
  mangabeys 7: 386–387
  marmosets and tamarins
    (SEE marmosets and
    tamarins)
  muriqui 4: 180–181; 9: 536
  proboscis 6: *301*, 302;
    7: 386, *386*
  rhesus 7: 388
  spider 2: 79, *79*; 7: 385
  spot-nosed 8: *459*
  squirrel 4: *204*; 7: 387;
    8: *469*

tamarins (SEE marmosets
  and tamarins)
  Thomas's leaf 6: 302
  titi 7: 387
  uakaris 7: 387
monkey puzzle trees 9: 516
monsoon forests 1: 22–23, 25;
  7: **389–390**, *389*; 9: 499,
  517, 518; 10: 551
monsoons 3: 114
Monte Azules Biosphere Reserve
  7: 369
Monteverde cloud forest 8: *478*
mora 9: 522
mosquitoes 2: 64, 89;
  3: 121–122, 150–151, *150*;
  5: 275, 291; 6: 304,
  306–307, 311; 7: 381, **391**,
  391; 8: 430; 10: 599
mosses 2: 100; 5: 240; 7: 390,
  392–393, *392–393*, 412;
  8: 449–452, *478*; 10: 571
  liverworts 7: 393
  Spanish 4: 184, *184*
moths 2: 69–73; 4: 205; 5: 275;
  6: 304–305, *307*,
  307–308, 313, 315;
  7: 410; 8: 460–461
  (SEE ALSO butterflies
  and moths)
  emperors 6: 304
  hawk moths 6: 307; 8: 424
  silk moths 2: 69, 72–73;
    6: 307, *307*
  uraniids 2: 73, *73*
mountain ebony 7: 390
mud slides 4: 188
mudskippers (SEE fish)
Myanmar 1: 22; 4: 189; 6: 343;
  10: 550
mycorrhizae 7: 417; 8: 425;
  10: 553, 572

national parks 1: 2; 3: 125–126,
  128–129; 6: 303;
  7: 389–390, **395–400**;
  9: 496; 10: 551, 559
  Bwindi Impenetrable Forest

  7: *399*; 8: *452*
  Chitwan 7: 395, 397
  Cross River 7: 399
  Dzanga-Ndoki 3: 129
  Eungella 1: 27
  Gombe Stream 1: 2
  Guatopo 7: 397
  Gunung Leuser 6: 303
  Kahuzi-Biega 3: 125
  Kerinci Sablat 6: 303;
    7: 397
  Khao Yai 7: *395*, 397
  Korup 7: 395, 398–399
  Kuna Indian Forest Park
    7: 396
  La Amistad 7: 400
  Lamington 7: 399
  Manú 4: 194; 7: 399–400,
    400
  Masaola 6: 349
  Olympic 7: *392*, 399, 413;
    9: *507*
  Periyar 7: 389, *389*, 397
  Ranomafana 7: 396, *396*
  Taman Negara 7: 397, *397*
  Tamborine 1: *26*
  Ujung Kulon 6: 303; 9: 498
  Xingu 6: 319; 9: 496
  Yasuni 7: 417
natural selection 7: **401–402**
naturalists 3: 127–128
nectar 2: 56–57, 70, 71, 88;
  3: 116; 4: 190, 205
Nepal 1: 22
nest and nest-building 2: 60–63,
  79, 96; 3: 163; 7: **403–405**,
  403–405; 10: 560–561, 577
New Guinea 4: 190; 6: 300;
  7: 416; 10: 581
New Zealand 7: 406, *406*;
  8: 476; 10: 556
newts 10: 593
Nicaragua 2: 98–99
Nigeria 1: 3; 3: 146; 4: 195;
  6: 342
Nigerian Conservation
  Foundation 4: 201
nightjars 7: 410

Boldface numbers before colons indicate volumes; **boldface** numbers following colons indicate whole articles; *italic* numbers are the page numbers of illustrations.

nocturnal animals **3**: 120, 130, 140; **7**: **407–410**; **8**: **426–427**, 469

North America **2**: 90; **7**: **411–413**, *411*; **10**: 556–559

numbats **4**: 207

nurse logs **7**: 412

nutmeg **7**: 390

nutrient cycle **7**: **414–415**, *414*

nutrients **4**: 184, 186–188, 195, 204–205, 209, 231–233; **6**: 305, 314–315, 330; **7**: 362-363, 414–415; **9**: 501, 507–509, 519–520, 525; **10**: 553, 572–573, 582, 585, 600

oil exploration **4**: 181; **5**: 283; **7**: **416–417**; **8**: 463–464; **9**: 496

okapis **1**: 28, 45; **3**: 125; **4**: 205; **6**: 355; **7**: **418**, *418*

okoume **1**: 4

Olympic National Park (SEE national parks)

Omere Wiki Foundation **2**: 101

omnivores **4**: 231–232; **6**: 355

oranges **4**: 227

orangutans **1**: 16–18; **3**: 163; **4**: *177*, 178; **6**: 302–303; **7**: 405, **419**, *419*

orchids **2**: 78, 99–100; **3**: 162; **4**: 183–184, 189, 222, 227, 229; **5**: 285; **7**: 390; **8**: **424–425**, *424–425*, 459–460; **9**: 507–508, 510, 519, 521, 536; **10**: 552, 571, 581

    Christmas star **8**: 424

    Dendrophylax **8**: 425

Orinoco River **7**: 376, 417; **10**: 604

Orinoco River basin **4**: 217–218

oropendolas **7**: 403, 405; **10**: 554

    chestnut-headed **7**: *404*

otters **7**: 399, 412; **9**: 502;

10: 595

giant otters (SEE giant otters)

ovenbirds **7**: 405

owls **2**: 56, 60; **4**: 207; **7**: 407–410, 412; **8**: **426–427**

    Australian masked **8**: 426

    eagle **2**: 60–61

    fishing **8**: 427

    great gray **2**: 60

    great horned **8**: 426

    Papuan hawk **8**: 427

    least pygmy **8**: 426–427

    lesser sooty **8**: 426

    Madagascar red **6**: 349

    sooty **7**: *409*; **8**: 426

    spectacled **8**: 427, *427*

    spotted **2**: 61; **4**: 182, *182*; **10**: 558

    Sumatran scops **6**: 303

    tropical screech **8**: *426*

    Verreux's eagle **2**: 59

Pacific islands **10**: 556, 558, 581

pademelons, red-necked **10**: 551, *551*

palms **1**: 24; **8**: **428–429**, *477*; **9**: 509, 520, *521*, 522; **10**: 590, *590*

    bottle **4**: 190

    climbing **3**: 116–117

    coco de mer **9**: 519

    coconut **8**: 428–429

    date **8**: 428

    nipa **7**: 362

    oil **1**: 4; **3**: 124; **4**: 226, *226*; **8**: 428–429, *428*, 454

    rattans (SEE rattans)

    sago **4**: 228; **5**: 289, *289*; **8**: 429, *429*

    talipot **8**: 428–429

Panama **1**: 43; **2**: 98–99

Panama Canal **7**: 391; **10**: 599

Panara people **9**: 496

Pangaea **4**: 189

pangolins **4**: 207; **10**: 571

papayas, or pawpaw, or papaw **4**: 229

Papua New Guinea **4**: 189

Paraguay **2**: 108; **9**: 535; **10**: 550, *550*, 552

parallel evolution **6**: 309

parasites **3**: 150–151; **6**: 307–308, 314; **8**: **430–431**, *430–431*, 449

    Amyema **8**: 430

    Bilharzia **8**: 430–431

    Ichneumons **8**: *430*, 431

    mistletoes **8**: 430–431, *431*

park rangers **2**: 82–83; **4**: 181

Parkia **4**: 221

parrots **1**: 4; **2**: 58, *58*, 61–63; **4**: 203, 206; **5**: 241, 276; **7**: 400; **8**: **432–434**; **10**: 571

    African gray **3**: 125; **8**: 432

    Amazon **8**: *433*

    cockatoos (SEE cockatoos)

    crimson rosella **7**: 399

    eclectus **8**: 432

    great-billed **8**: 434

    king **8**: 434

    lories **8**: 432–434

    lorikeets **8**: 432–434

        rainbow **8**: 434, *434*

    macaws (SEE macaws)

    palm parakeets **8**: 433

    Puerto Rican **4**: *203*

    red-sided **2**: 61

passionflowers **4**: 220; **8**: *449*, 450, 452

passionfruit **4**: 229, *232*

peanuts **4**: 230

peccaries **2**: 75, 100; **3**: 165; **4**: 232; **6**: 355–356 (SEE ALSO pigs and peccaries)

Penan people (SEE Punan, or Penan people)

people of the rain forest **8**: **435–442** (for groups, see individual entries)

peperomias **9**: 509

peppers **4**: 229

Boldface numbers before colons indicate volumes; boldface numbers following colons indicate whole articles; *italic* numbers are the page numbers of illustrations.

Peru **1**: 6, 20–21, 43–44; **4**: 194; **7**: 417

Philippines **1**: 22–23; **2**: 64, 108; **3**: 146; **4**: 177, 189, 195, 216; **7**: 416; **9**: 496

photosynthesis **2**: 64, 80–81; **3**: 115; **6**: 323, 328–329; **8**: 425, 431, **443–444**, *443*, 449–450; **9**: 509–510, 519–520, 523–524; **10**: 553, 572, 574

Piaroa people **4**: *195*; **5**: 281, *281*; **8**: 438–439, *439*

pigeons **2**: 57, 61; **3**: 133; **5**: 273

pigs and peccaries **5**: 276; **8**: **445–446**; **9**: 526 (SEE ALSO peccaries)
> babirusas (SEE babirusas)
> bearded pigs **7**: 376, *376*; **8**: 445
> collared peccaries **8**: 446
> giant forest hogs **8**: 446, *446*
> red river hogs **8**: *458*
> white-lipped peccaries **8**: 446

pineapples **4**: 229; **5**: 251

pines **7**: 390, 406
> matai, or black pine **7**: 406; **8**: 476
> rimu, or red pine **7**: 406; **8**: 476

piranhas **4**: 210–211 **8**: **447**, *447*, 465

pirarucus **4**: 211; **8**: **448**, *448*

pitcher plants **1**: 24, 28; **2**: **88–89**, *88*
> phial pitcher **2**: 89
> raja pitcher **2**: 88
> yellow trumpet **2**: 89

pittas **2**: 59; **5**: 241; **10**: 595
> rainbow **7**: 405
> Shneider's **6**: 303

plantations **1**: 4, 21; **4**: 176, 178; **6**: 301; **7**: 373; **8**: 428, 429, **454–455**, *454–455*; **9**: 486, 496–497, 511–512;

10: 559, 575
> banana **2**: 99–100, *101*; **8**: *454*
> cacao **4**: 229
> oil palm **4**: 178, 181, 226
> rubber **4**: 178, 196, *196*
> tree **3**: 128, 147, 171; **8**: *455*

plants, general **8**: 443–444, **449–453**; **9**: 523–524, 536 (for species, see individual entries)

plum trees **7**: 390

poaching **2**: 63, 109; **3**: 128; **4**: 178–179; **5**: 282; **7**: 418; **8**: **456–459**, *456–459*

podologists **2**: 82

poisons **7**: 377; **9**: 502, 507, 510, 513–514, 519–520, 522, 531–532; **10**: 561, 575, 577, 583–584

pollination **2**: 56–57, 64, 78; **3**: 128, 162–163; **4**: 190, 196, 219–222; **6**: 305, 315; **8**: 424–425, 431, **460–462**, *460–462*, 479; **10**: 572

pollution **3**: 152; **5**: 238, 283, *283*; **7**: 379, 417; **8**: **463–465**, *463–465*; **9**: 487, 496; **10**: 599, 605

porcupines (SEE rodents)

porpoises **10**: 595

possums and opossums **6**: 353, 355; **7**: 399, 408; **8**: **466–467**
> gliding possums **8**: 467, *467*
> honey possums **3**: 163; **4**: 205; **5**: 273, 276; **6**: 353
> lutrine opossums **8**: 467
> mouse opossums **6**: *353*
> pygmy possums **8**: 466
> ring-tailed possums **8**: 467
> spotted cuscuses **8**: *466*, 467
> water opossums **8**: 467

prawns (SEE crustaceans)

praying mantises (SEE mantises)

primates **1**: 7, 25, 45; **7**: 398, 400, 405; **8**: **468–470**, *468–470*; **10**: 552, 557, 595 (for species, see individual entries)

puffbirds **6**: 308

puma **2**: 90–91

Punan, or Penan people **8**: 436–437, 480

pythons (SEE snakes)

Queensland **1**: 26–27

quetzals, resplendent **2**: 61, *61*, 99; **5**: 251, 274; **7**: 400; **8**: 478; **10**: 571

Quinault people **8**: **471–472**, *471–472*

Quinault rain forest **8**: *471*

quinine **4**: 196

quolls, spotted tail **7**: 408

rabbits **1**: 28; **10**: 553

raccoons **10**: 571

rafflesias **1**: 24; **4**: 220; **8**: 431, 451, **473**, *473*; **9**: 520

rain forests **8**: **474–478**
> structure **8**: 474, *474*
> types of **8**: 475–478

rainfall **3**: 114–115, *115*, 124, 164, 167; **4**: 186–188; **5**: 284–285, 290; **7**: 389–390, 406, 411; **9**: 499, 515, 517–518, 534–535; **10**: 551, 556, 558, 580–583, 597–598, 600–601

rambutans **4**: 227; **5**: *250*; **9**: 520

rata **7**: 406; **8**: 476

rattans **1**: 24; **3**: 117; **8**: 428, **479–480**, *479–480*

red cedars **10**: 557

red pandas **8**: **481**, *481*

reforestation **2**: 101; **4**: 188, *188*; **5**: 263; **9**: **486–489**

reptiles, general **3**: 118–119, 134–137; **9**: **490–493**;

Boldface numbers before colons indicate volumes; **boldface** numbers following colons indicate whole articles; *italic* numbers are the page numbers of illustrations.

10: 594 (for species, see individual entries)

research (SEE exploration and research)

resettlement **2**: 94–95; **6**: 319; **9**: 494–497

rhinoceroses **1**: 25; **5**: 274; **6**: 302–303; **9**: 498; **10**: 551, 583

Javan **4**: 178; **6**: 302; **9**: 498

Sumatran **4**: 178–179, *178*; **6**: 302; **9**: 498, *498*

rice **4**: 228

rivers **3**: 130, 152; **9**: 499–502, *499–500*, 518; **10**: 598–601

road building **3**: 129, 148; **4**: 181, 186–187, 195; **6**: 341, 342, 343; **9**: 496

rodents **9**: 503–506, 536; **10**: 548–549, 558

agoutis **9**: 503–504, 536

capybaras (SEE capybaras)

guinea pigs **9**: 504, 506

mice **7**: 408; **9**: 504–506

pencil-tailed tree **9**: 505

pacas **9**: *503*, 504, 536

porcupines **9**: 503–506

tree porcupine, or coendou **9**: *506*

rats **9**: 504–506

naked-tailed climbing **9**: *505*

swamp **9**: 505

water **9**: 505

shrews **6**: 308–309; **7**: 410

tree shrews **3**: 123, 133; **6**: *356*

squirrels (SEE squirrels)

voles, red-backed **7**: 412

Rondônia **1**: 7; **4**: 180

roots **7**: 362–363; **9**: 507–510; **10**: 549, 553, 571, 573, 581, 597–598

rose mahogany **10**: 551

rose satinash **10**: 551

rosy periwinkle **2**: 54–55; **4**: 196; **7**: 375, *375*

rubber **1**: 4; **3**: 147; **8**: 454;

9: 496–497, **511–512**, *511–512*

Rwanda **4**: 201

saffron heart **10**: 551

salamanders **1**: 8; **2**: 79; **6**: 339; **9**: *513*, 516; **10**: 571, 593, 598–599, *599*

salmon (SEE fish)

salmonella **1**: 28

sandalwood **7**: 390; **8**: 459

sapele (African mahogany) **1**: 3–4; **3**: 124, 146, 171; **10**: 575

sapodilla **4**: 225–226

scarlet ibis **7**: 363

scarlet minivet **7**: 397

scavengers **4**: 233; **5**: 240–241

scientific research **2**: 76–77, 82–83

scorpions **2**: 79; **5**: 241; **9**: **514**, *514*

scrub turkeys **10**: 551

scythebills **4**: 207

seasons **2**: 78; **7**: 376, 389–390; **9**: 499, 515–518; **10**: 548, 550–552, 556–558, 573

seed dispersal **5**: 250–251

seeds **2**: 56–58, 61; **9**: 488, **519–522**, 524, 536; **10**: 557, 573–574, 584–585

Semang people **5**: 289; **8**: 436

Sepilok Rehabilitation Center **4**: *177*, 178

shade toleration **3**: 162; **6**: 324; **9**: **523–524**

Shorea **10**: 572

shrikes **4**: 207

shrimp (SEE crustaceans)

Sierra Leone **1**: 3; **4**: 216

sifakas (SEE lemurs)

Sitka spruce **3**: 153; **7**: 412; **10**: 557

skinks **6**: 335

blue-tongued **6**: 335

Brazilian **6**: 334

marine **6**: 333

Murray's forest **1**: 27

orange-sided **1**: 27

slash and burn **1**: 4, 21; **3**: 147; **4**: 187, 195; **5**: 262, 292; **6**: 321, 348; **7**: 368, 380; **8**: 464; **9**: **525–526**, *525–526*; **10**: 604

sloths **2**: 79, 100; **3**: 163; **6**: 354, 356; **9**: 527, *527*; **10**: 554, *554*

slugs **4**: 233 (SEE ALSO slugs and snails)

Veronicella **9**: 529

slugs and snails **6**: 310–312; **9**: **528–529**, *528–529*

snails **2**: 64; **4**: 217, 233; **5**: 240; **7**: 410; **10**: 572

Achatina fulica **9**: 528–529

Papustyla **9**: 529

(SEE ALSO slugs and snails)

snakes **4**: 206; **6**: 336, 338; **7**: 407–408; **9**: 490–493, **530–533**; **10**: 571, 594

anaconda **2**: 84, *85*; **3**: 130; **9**: 530

blind **9**: 531

boa **3**: 130–131; **4**: 232; **7**: 407–408; **9**: 531

rainbow **3**: *130*, 131

bushmasters **9**: 530, 532

camouflage **2**: 75; **3**: 131

cobras **3**: **118–119**; **9**: 531–532

king cobras **1**: 25; *118–119*; **9**: 490, 533

constrictors **3**: **130–131**

coral **9**: 492, *531*, 532

fer-de-lance **9**: *492*, 493, 531

flowerpot **9**: 530

flying **9**: 533

kraits **3**: 119

mussuranas **9**: 531

nesting **3**: 119

parrot **9**: *530*

pipe **9**: 532

Boldface numbers before colons indicate volumes; **boldface** numbers following colons indicate whole articles; *italic* numbers are the page numbers of illustrations.

snakes (cont.)
  pythons **2:** 84; **3:** 119,
      130–131; **4:** 232;
      9: 491, 530–533, *533*
    green tree **3:** 131, *131*
    Indian **3:** 130; **9:** 531,
      533
    reticulated **1:** *24,* 25;
      9: 531
    ringed **3:** 131
    rat **3:** 119
    tree **9:** 532–533
    venom **3:** 118–119
    vine **9:** 530, 532,
      532
  vipers **9:** 531, 533
    eyelash **5:** 287; **9:** *491*
    gaboon **1:** 5, *5;*
      3: 125; **9:** 493
    jumping **9:** 530
    lichen **9:** 492
soil **2:** 76, 88, 94–95, 100–101,
    109; **3:** 148, 167;
    4: 186–187, 195; **5:** 241,
    243–244; **9:** 486–487, 494,
    501, 507–509, 525–526;
    10: 582
Sonneratia **7:** 362
South America **1:** 44; **2:** 94;
    4: 179–180, 189–190, 215,
    217; **9:** 496, **534–538;**
    10: 552, 581
Southeast Asia **3:** 146, 148;
    4: 177
spices **4:** 227–228; **5:** **271–272,**
    10: 575
  cinnamon **4:** 227; **5:** 272
  cloves **4:** 227; **5:** 271, 272
  ginger **4:** 227; **5:** 272
  mace **4:** 227
  nutmeg **4:** 227; **5:** 272
  pepper **4:** 227; **5:** 271–272
  vanilla **4:** 229; **5:** 272, *272;*
    8: 424
spiders **2:** 74–75, 79, 89; **3:** 122;
    4: 205, 217; **5:** 241;
    6: 308–310, 315;
    7: 408–409; **9:** **539–543;**

    10: 572, 581
  bolas **9:** 541
  crab **6:** *308;* **9:** 542–543,
      542
  Curimagua **9:** 539
  gladiator **9:** 543
  goliath bird-eating
      tarantulas **6:** 310; **9:** 539,
      541, *543*
  jumping **9:** 542–543
    orsima ichneumon **9:** 542
  net-casting **7:** *410*
  nursery web **6:** 315
  orb web **9:** 540
    Gasteracantha **9:** 540
    golden orb web **9:** *540*
    Nephila **9** : 540
  red kite **9:** *539*
  trap-door **9:** 542
    Liphistius, giant trap-door
      9: *541,* 542
  wolf **9:** 543
squirrels **5:** 273; **6:** 337, 354;
    7: 390, 403, 412;
    9: 503–506;
    10: **548–549,** 551, 571
  Douglas **10:** *548*
  flying **1:** 25; **6:** 338; **7:** 399;
    9: 505, 516; **10:** 549,
    558, 595
      northern **7:** 412, *412*
  Malabar **7:** 397
  marmots **10:** 548, *549*
  pygmy **10:** 548
  scaly-tailed **9:** 505;
    African **10:** 549
Sri Lanka **10:** 581
Stanley, Henry Morton **4:**
    199, *199*
strangler figs **3:** 117; **8:** 451;
    9: 507, 509; **10:** 585, *585*
subtropical rain forests **9:** 517,
    535; **10:** **550–552,** 573
succession **5:** 243
sugarcane **1:** 45; **4:** 228
Sulawesi **4:** 179; **6:** 300–302
Sumatra **4:** 178; **6:** 300–301,
    303; **9:** *525*

sunbirds **2:** 56–57; **4:** 205;
    5: 273; **7:** 376; **10:** 594
sundri **7:** 362
swallows **6:** 308
sweet potatoes **4:** 230
swifts **6:** 308; **7:** 405
  Asian palm **7:** 405
Swiss-cheese plants **3:** 117;
    9: 509, 520; **10:** 591
symbiosis **7:** 415;
    10: **553–554**

tailorbirds **7:** 404
Taiwan **10:** 550
tanagers **10:** 595
Tanzania **1:** 2
tapirs **2:** 100; **3:** 165; **4:** 179,
    204; **5:** 274, 275; **7:** 398;
    10: 553, **555,** *555,* 583
tarsiers **6:** 302, *302;*
    8: 468–469
teak **3:** 146–147, 171; **4:** 194;
    6: 331, 340, 342; **7:** 389;
    8: 455, *455;* **9:** *488,* 518;
    10: 575
temperate rain forests **2:** 53, 60,
    90, 108–109; **3:** 114–115,
    165; **7:** 411–413;
    9: 515–516, 535;
    10: 548–549, **556–559,**
    564–566, 569
temperature **3:** 114–115
tenrecs **4:** 207; **10:** 595
termites **1:** 28; **3:** 140, 163;
    4: 204, 232; **5:** 240, 274;
    6: 305, 307, 313;
    7: 403–404; **10:** 553–554,
    560–561, *560–561,* 571,
    582
    Macrotermes **10:** *560,* 561
Thailand **1:** 22–23; **3:** 146;
    4: 188–189; **6:** 342–343;
    9: 496
thismia **4:** 220
thrips **4:** 221
tierra firme forest **1:** 6
tigers **1:** 25, *25;* **2:** 84, 86,
    90–92; **3:** 133; **6:** 302–303;

Boldface numbers before colons indicate volumes; **boldface** numbers following colons indicate whole articles; *italic* numbers are the page numbers of illustrations.

668

7: 363, 390, 397, 408–409;
10: 562–563, *562–563*

Tikuna people 4: 215–216;
8: 440

Tlingit people 10: 564–565,
564–565

toads, general (SEE ALSO frogs
and toads)
African clawed 1: 9
fire-bellied 1: 9
giant, or cane 4: 233;
5: 246, 249, *249*
golden 2: 99, *99*
horned 1: 9
Surinam, or pipa 1: 9;
5: 248

tortoises (SEE turtles and
terrapins)

toucans 3: 123; 5: 273, 276;
9: 518, 538, *538*;
10: 566–567, 594
groove-billed toucanets
10: *567*
keel-billed 10: *566*
toco 10: 552

tourism 2: 82–83, 99, 101
3: 128–129, 137;
4: 182; 5: 245, 266, 280,
282; 7: 396–400; 8: 458,
463; 9: 537; 10: 568–569

transmigration 6: 301

tree creepers 10: 558

tree ferns 10: 575

tree frogs (SEE frogs)

tree kangaroos (SEE kangaroos)

tree nurseries 9: *486*, 487–489,
488–489

trees 7: 389; 9: 486–489, 501,
507–510, 516–522;
10: 549, 551, 553, 557,
559, 570–575, 590 (for
species, see individual
entries)
hardwoods 3: 124–125,
128, 146, 148–149
softwoods 3: 147

Tropical Forest Research Centre
4: 201

Tropical Forestry Action Plan
4: 201

tropical rain forest 10: 580–585,
580, 582
lowland 10: 580

truffles 10: 549

tualangs 3: 171; 10: 572

turacos 10: 595

turtles and terrapins 3: 141;
4: 181; 9: 490–491, 493,
502; 10: 586–589, 594
African hingeback 10: 587
arau river 10: 588
Chinese box 10: *589*
Cuora box 10: 587
hinge-backed tortoises
9: *491*
matamata 10: *587*
mud 10: 587–588
scorpion mud 10: *588*
musk 10: 589
red-eared terrapins 10: *586,*
589
river 4: 181
sidenecked, or
snake-necked 10: 587
snapping 10: 588
softshells 10: 588
spiny hill tortoises 9: 493,
493
yellow-footed tortoises
4: 181

Twa people 1: 3; 3: 125

typhoid 1: 28

tyrant flycatchers 7: 376

Uganda 1: 3

understory 2: 76, 100; 10: 571,
585, 590–591

underwater plants 8: 452
571, 585, 590–591

United Nations 9: 487

United Nations Environment
Programme 3: 127

United States 3: 115

upas trees 5: 289

utile 1: 3

U'wa people 7: 417

vanilla 8: 424

varzea forest 1: 7

Venezuela 4: 195, 199;
10: 604–605

vertebrates 10: 592–595

Vietnam 1: 22; 4: 189

violets, African 1: 3; 8: 444

vipers (SEE snakes)

vultures 3: 141; 10: 596
king *596*

Wallace's line 6: 300

Wanariset Research Institute for
Sustainable Forestry 9: *487*

warblers 2: 58; 6: 308; 7: 376

Warrau people 5: 289; 8: *440*

wasps 1: 34–36; 7: *403, 405*;
10: 554, 581, 591 (SEE
ALSO bees and wasps)
paper 7: 403
potter 7: 403
tiger hornet 1: 36
yellow jackets 1: 36
Zethus 1: 36

water 3: 114–115; 9: 499,
501–502, 518; 10: 583,
597–599

water cycle 5: 284–285

watershed 7: 397;
10: 600–601, *601*

weevils, toothpick 10: 552

West Indies 10: 581

western hemlock 7: 412;
10: 557

western red cedar 7: 412

Wet Tropics World Heritage Area
1: 27

whip scorpions 2: 96; 5: 241

white beefwood 10: 551

wild pine sergeants 2: 59

Wildlife Conservation
International 4: 201

wood hoopoes 2: 59

wood ibises 7: 376

wood storks 7: 376

woodcreepers 2: 59

woodpeckers 2: 58–59, 61;
4: 204, 207; 6: 309, 337;

Numbers in **bold** indicate volumes; page numbers in *italic* indicate illustrations; page numbers in **bold** refer to full articles.

woodpeckers (cont.)
  7: 389, 412; **10**: 558, 571
  crimson-winged **2**: *59*
World Conservation Monitoring
  Centre **3**: 127; **4**: 176
World Conservation Union
  (IUCN) **3**: 127; **4**: 201
World Forestry Congress **4**: 201
World Wide Fund for Nature
  (WWF) **3**: 127, 129; **4**: 201
worms **3**: 140, 151; **4**: 217, 233;
  6: 310, 312–313,
  336–337; **10**: 572,
  598–599, **602–603**,
  602–603
  velvet **2**: 99; **6**: 312, *312*,
  315; **10**: 603

Xingu National Park (SEE
  national parks)

yams **4**: 228
Yanomami people **3**: 149,
  151; **5**: 280; **8**: 438–440;
  10: **604–605**, *604–605*
yellow fever **7**: 391
yellow-green vireos **7**: 376
Yoruba people **5**: 279–280,
  292

zoologists **2**: 82–83

Boldface numbers before colons indicate volumes; **boldface** numbers following colons indicate whole articles; *italic* numbers are the page numbers of illustrations.